SpringerBriefs in Finance

More information about this series at http://www.springer.com/series/10282

Henry Schäfer

On Values in Finance and Ethics

Forgotten Trails and Promising Pathways

Springer

Henry Schäfer
Institute of Business Administration
University of Stuttgart
Stuttgart, Germany

ISSN 2193-1720 ISSN 2193-1739 (electronic)
SpringerBriefs in Finance
ISBN 978-3-030-04683-5 ISBN 978-3-030-04684-2 (eBook)
https://doi.org/10.1007/978-3-030-04684-2

Library of Congress Control Number: 2018965162

This Springer imprint is published by the registered company Springer Nature Switzerland AG
The registered company address is: Gewerbestrasse 11, 6330 Cham, Switzerland

Preface

Sustainable investments, socially responsible investments, impact investings, green finance, blended finance, and many other buzzwords that are resounding throughout the world suggest that financial matters have undergone a welcome reform into a brave new world. But has the financial sector really recalled old virtues and rediscovered forgotten trails of ethics and morality? Do global challenges like climate change and other violations of a sustainable global development offer promising pathways for an ethical renaissance within the financial sector?

The book at hand is intended to shed more light on such issues. It opens with the building blocks of modern capital market theory as the starting point for the analysis of a hidden ethical content, or even the foundations of current capital market and finance theory. Later the long-standing struggle between ethics and economics is demonstrated, which illustrates how the alienation between the financial and the real side of economies and economic relationships can be explained. A brief introduction into the basic pillars of ethics and morality is presented and linked with selected standard models of modern capital market theory and finance theory. The sustainability development approach is demonstrated as having the potential to initiate a scientific revolution in finance according to *Kuhn's* methodological approach. Furthermore, a roadmap of modern value thinking, i.e., sustainability, corporate social responsibility, and the theory of external effects, is elaborated. The book then proceeds with the crucial role of stakeholders and nongovernmental organizations in coping with firm behavior combatting sustainability and responsibility. Contractual relationships between these groups and the role of the "license to operate" in a de facto borderless global world are also discussed. The book ends with a critical reflection of selected issues for a sustainability-linked finance that demonstrate the still nascent state of ethics and finance.

Stuttgart, Germany — Henry Schäfer

Preface

Contents

Abbreviations

ADM	Arrow, Debreu and McKenzie
APT	Arbitrage pricing theory
bn	Billion
CAPM	Capital asset pricing model
CF(s)	Cash flow(s)
CFP	Corporate financial performance
CIC	Codex Iuris Canonici
COP	Conference of the parties
CSP	Corporate social performance
CSR	Corporate social responsibility
EC	European Commission
ESG	Environmental, social, governance
EU	European Union
EU-ETS	Emission Trading scheme of the European Union
EURIBOR	Euro Interbank Offered Rate
GRI	Global Reporting Initiative
IPCC	Intergovernmental Panel on Climate Change
LIBOR	London Interbank Offered Rate
m	Million
MEH	Market efficiency hypothesis
MIT	Massachusetts Institute of Technology
MM	Modigliani and Miller
MNC	Multinational Company
MU	Monetary unit
NGO	Nongovernmental organization
OECD	Organisation for Economic Co-operation and Development
Ph.D.	Philosophiae Doctor = Doctor of Philosophy
PRI	Principles for Responsible Investments
R&D	Research and development
REH	Rational expectation hypothesis

SDG	Sustainable development goals
SocGen	Société Générale
SRI	Socially responsible investments
TCFD	Task Force on Climate-Related Financial Disclosures
TOC	Transnational Organized Crime
trn	Trillion
UBS	Union Bank of Switzerland
UK	United Kingdom
UN	United Nations
UNCED	United Nations Conference on Environment and Development
UNEP FI	UN Environment Programme for the Finance Initiative
USD	US-Dollar
WACC	Weighted average cost of capital
WBCSD	World Business Council of Sustainable Development
WCED	World Commission of Environment and Development

Notations

a	A set of possible actions $a = (1,2,\ldots,A)$
c (a,s)	A set of consequences resulting from the interaction of activities and the state of the world
DC	Damage cost
DU	Damage unit
E (.)	Expectation operator
I	Investment
i	Asset
MC	Marginal cost
MD	Marginal damage
$\theta(s)$	Probability distribution function
$P_{i,t}$	Market price of an asset i
p^0	Initial price of a good
p^*	Price of a good due to internalized negative external effects
q_i	Weight of an asset i
r	Rate of return
s	Set of future states of the environment $s = (1,2,\ldots,S)$
tx	*Pigou* tax
t	Time
$u(c)$	Utility function
V	Money value
W	Market value
x	Quantity of goods
Z_i	Present value of a cash flow of an asset i
€	Euro
ϕ	Information vector

List of Figures

Chapter 1
Introduction

Abstract Over the last four decades, finance and capital markets have experienced tremendous progress in producing theoretical models and their applications in practice. At the beginning of this process, financial innovations served as very helpful tools for coping with risks and earning sound money. Lately, due to the banking and subprime crisis, doubts have arisen about the capability of finance and capital markets to serve as enablers for easing economic transactions in the real part of the economy, contributing to the welfare of societies, and, last but not least, to being legitimized as an integral part of a capitalistic system. Deep ethical concerns about the shortcomings and necessary improvements to financial systems and their participants have occupied not only regulators but also media, politicians, and stakeholders. What we are still missing is a broad reflection of ethics in finance and capital market theory. The following chapter introduces the structure of this book and the major topics that it tackles.

Keywords Financial crisis · Financial innovation · Unethical behavior · Ignorance · Ethics · Morality

> You can check-out any time you like. But you can never leave![1]

These are the last two sentences of the title track of the album *Hotel California* released in February 1976 by the world-famous Californian country pop band *The Eagles*. As one of the text writers later explained, the whole song is about the underbelly of the American dream and about excessive ways of living in industrialized countries. Since the song's fantastic career as a *shooting star in the top ten charts* in many countries, *tremendous innovations in technologies* and ways of *living* have been established, revolutionizing economies, societies, and nature. It is

---

The original version of this chapter was revised. A correction to this chapter is available at https://doi.org/10.1007/978-3-030-04684-2_8.

[1] https://www.azlyrics.com/lyrics/eagles/hotelcalifornia.html

H. Schäfer, *On Values in Finance and Ethics*, SpringerBriefs in Finance,
https://doi.org/10.1007/978-3-030-04684-2_1

remarkable that some of the most important drivers of these ongoing developments can also be dated back to the mid-1970s. For instance, *Steve Jobs*, *Steve Wozniak*, and *Ronald Wayne* founded Apple Inc., and *Bill Gates* together with *Paul Allen* laid the foundations of the terrific career of Microsoft Inc. Both *ventures* earmark the beginning of *fundamental* technological and business *innovations that* has dramatically *changed the world* over the last nearly four decades—even in the world of finance, banking, and capital markets.

What has happened in the world of finance in the 1970s? It can best be illustrated by some selected innovation highlights like the *Black/Scholes* formula (Black and Scholes 1973) which began a revolution in capital markets. It was accompanied by extensions of option pricing modellings like the *Cox/Ross/Rubinstein* binominal model (Cox et al. 1979) and not to forget the arbitrage pricing theory published by *Ross* (1976) as an alternative valuation model to the capital asset pricing model. That means that parallel to the innovations within the real sectors of the economy, the *financial sector* also initiated *groundbreaking innovations*. At the time only few people will have been aware of the dramatic potential in the level playing field in nearly every part of life and that finance was standing at the dawn of a historically outstanding career.

Finance became the enabler of technical innovations, start-ups, and fitness programs for frozen firm conglomerates. But in many countries, the financial industry also created *financial innovations for their own*. Intransparent financial vehicles like conduits, rocket science-based investment products and risk tools, ultrahigh-speed tradings in securities exchanges, etc. are only the tip of an iceberg of dynamic forces in the financial sector that frequently only a few agents have understood. These innovation processes came to an abrupt end with the *subprime* and the following *banking crisis* shortly after the start of the millennium. Questions were raised about how *excess speculation*, *selfish capital market participants*, and *untamed profit seeking* in the financial industry could arise and loosen the former close ties to the real sector and society. Among its audience and in finance in general, the crisis also caused concern about the *loss of any ethical or moral barriers* in capital markets.

In the movie *Wall Street 2*, the mature investment banker *Gordon Gekko* explained to his career-obsessed young partner that the financial crisis had demonstrated that "*money is a bitch*," i.e., finance is an unethical and amoral affair. In those times the media, nongovernmental organizations (e.g., Occupy), and politicians condemned the financial sector for its unethical behavior, its sangfroid, and its irresponsibility. The financial industry itself and its academic servants had deigned to accept criticism concerning violations of ethics and morality. An illustrative example is an event at the annual meeting of Nobel laureates at Lake Constance in Germany. The holder of the Nobel Prize for economics 1997, *Robert C. Merton*, was asked by a young researcher from the central bank of Indonesia what role Nobel laureates in economics played in the last financial crises. *Merton* himself wondered whether he had understood the question correctly, i.e., that it is his personal responsibility for the financial crisis. After uttering a big "Wow" on this "very complicated question," *Merton* elaborated on technical aspects of models in finance—not on ethical considerations what the asker might have meant.[2] Maybe the asker might have expected a comment in the sense of the following citation of a Swiss professor in banking and finance to a similar subject: "*This crisis is a moral crisis. Instruments and techniques can be used for the good or for its opposite. The mathematical models of finance we have developed do not include the human implications they lead to*" (Cossin 2009, p. 19).

Let us return to that song citation from the beginning. Following the past years of excess financial activities, the song citation should remind us that *finance sometimes checks out from the common "house of ethics and morality*," which is enveloping societies and economies as well as the human species. Ethics and morality guard against systems and institutions collapsing, as almost happened in the aftermath of the global financial crises. The crisis demonstrated that unethical behavior in capital markets can be a severe threat to societies and economies and the whole modern way of life.[3]

This is *not a book about the subprime and banking crisis,* although it starts with the most dramatic shortcomings of the financial industry over the past decades and continues with the necessity for ethical considerations in finance. The *pivotal idea* of the book is that, despite the "check-out hypothesis," *finance*, *financial activities*, and *financial agents* will *sooner or later be grounded in ethical virtue*. In other words, financial intermediaries cannot, in reality, leave the "*house of ethics and morality*." The reasons for this are addressed in this book. The core idea is that the former *close ties* between finance and ethics *have been forgotten*, *ignored*, *or abolished* —along with them the successful *auxiliary role of the financial sector* for the society, economy, and nature. However the rehabilitation of the link between finance and ethics is still possible and promises *new pathways* for a sustainable finance in general and capital markets in particular.

The book is organized as follows: it starts with the *building blocks of finance and modern capital market theory* (including behavioral finance) as the initial point for the analysis of the hidden ethical content or even the foundations of current capital market theory. A subsequent part demonstrates the long-standing *struggle between ethics and economics* of which finance is a part. It illustrates how these discussions can explain the alienation between the financial and the real side of economies and economic relationships. A brief introduction into the *basic pillars of ethics and morality* from a philosopher's point of view is presented, linked with the dominating standard models of modern capital markets and finance. It will be demonstrated that the *sustainable development approach* has the potential to initiate a scientific revolution in finance according to *Kuhn's* methodological approach.

---

[2]The original answer in full length is documented in a video available on https://www.mediatheque.lindau-nobel.org/videos/33985/2014-useful-economics/laureate-merton.

[3]When focusing on the relationship between ethics and finance in the following chapters of the book, one should not underestimate the very fundamental challenges of ethics in economics as *Taylor* (2014, p. 34) asked: "*Does the study of economics itself discourage moral behavior?*".

Furthermore a road map of *modern ethical value thinking*, i.e., sustainability, corporate social responsibility, and stakeholder theory, is elaborated. It proceeds with the crucial role of nongovernmental organizations in trying to cope with pitfalls of firm behavior that violates sustainability and responsibility. Contractual relationships between firms, capital market participants, and stakeholders and the role of the license to operate are discussed. The book finishes with a *sketch of* the *next generation of a value-linked financial and capital market* thinking—and their *challenges*.

Chapter 2
A "Selfie" of Finance and Ethics

Abstract Historically, finance and capital market theory have passed remarkable milestones. They have developed from a very practically minded tool box for the requirements of a firm's financial management to a highly sophisticated scientific discipline. The focus on mathematics, statistics, and physics has encouraged groundbreaking research in modern capital market theories. Without exaggeration it can be claimed that, for years, the research output of finance has outshone other research fields in economics and business administration. Financial economics have emerged in tandem with natural sciences, just as *Irving Fisher* and his followers have been sincerely wishing for. With the success of well-known capital market models in both practice and academia, the neoclassically based dichotomies between the real and the monetary sector have become fact. However, repeated crises in financial markets augmented a growing distrust for stakeholders, politicians, regulators, and media concerning the stability and efficiency of the financial sector. A growing awareness of and the demand for ethics and morality in financial markets has increased over the past decade. It has inspired new research that questions long-standing positions in finance but has still been unable to lay the groundwork for a new paradigm in finance and capital market theory that integrates ethics and morality within finance. Nevertheless the need to think and elaborate on finance and ethics remains.

Keywords Monetary theory · Capital market theory · Finance theory · Crisis · Stakeholder · Neoclassic · Financial crisis · Uncertainty · *Irving Fisher*

Capital market and finance theory have not simply arisen from nowhere. They have emerged historically along different paths of economic thought. Before modern capital market theory evolved in the 1920s with *Fisher's* paradigm of *value additivity* and the *separation theorem* (as described in the following Sect. 2.1), finance and capital markets were closely tied together. *Financial transactions* served as an *auxiliary* mean to enable the frictionless flow of goods and inventory piling. The basic reference model of a firm was the manufacturing entity, which combines productive factors (resources) as inputs to create outputs of marketable goods. Such a paradigm was widespread in the 1950s, and one of the well-known examples,

H. Schäfer, *On Values in Finance and Ethics*, SpringerBriefs in Finance,
https://doi.org/10.1007/978-3-030-04684-2_2

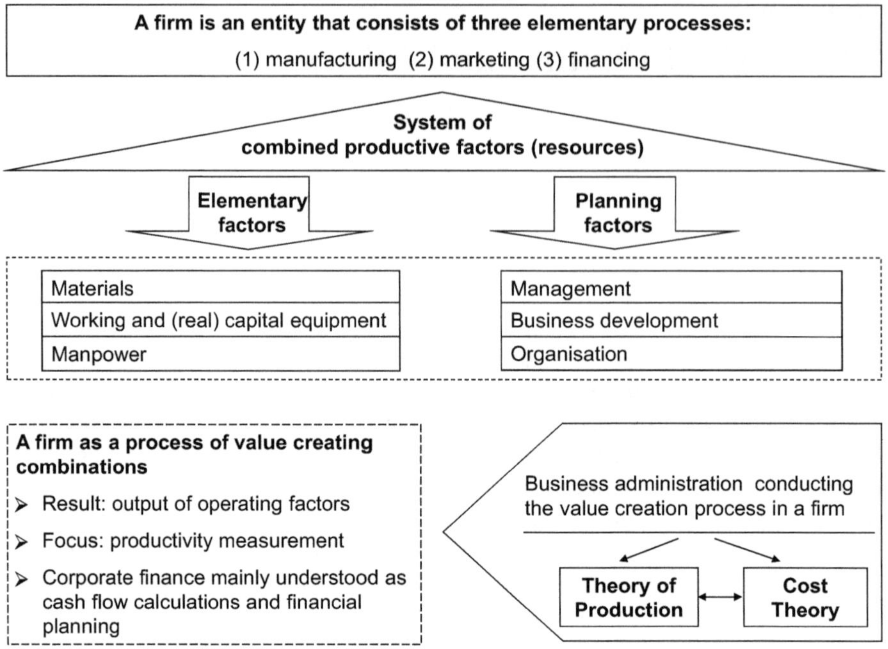

Fig. 2.1 A look back at the "old-fashioned world": finance and investment and its auxiliary role in the production model of *Erich Gutenberg*

not only in Germany, was *Gutenberg's* production theory and cost theory of the firm (Gutenberg 1958). The dominating view of a firm as a manufacturing entity operating in order to supply markets with goods that satisfy the urgent needs of demanding market participants emerged with the beginning of the industrial revolution in the nineteenth century. This concept can still be witnessed in modern thought as it describes most family-owned firms in many industrialized countries very well (Schäfer and Goldschmidt 2010, pp. 285–286).

According to such a *real economy-driven paradigm* (see Fig. 2.1), the main objectives of finance in practice as well as in academics were devoted to practical questions. Most often tackled subjects have been how to organize a firm's funding with short- and long-term capital, to ensuring the financial equilibrium of a firm (i.e., remaining solvent) and to managing special or stressful situations within firms such as the threat of a default, mergers, etc. For such purposes, finance had a very limited, special role to play and was reduced to financial management and closely linked to accounting and controlling. Academic representatives of such views were, among others, *Schmalenbach* (1922) in Germany and, in Anglo-Saxon countries, researchers like *Dewing* (1920), *Williams* (1938), and *Hoagland* (1933). Although such approaches were much closer to accounting than to microeconomics (see Fig. 2.2), *Solomon's* statement is intriguing: "The theory of financial management can be viewed as an extension of the theory of the firm. But whereas the traditional emphasis in microeconomics is on the relationship between profits and the volume of

Traditional view of finance

- Commodity driven view of the firm.
- A firm is represented by one or more entrepreneurs and seen as a homogenous decision-making entity with non-financial objectives.
- The focus of a firm is on production and sales (*Gutenberg* tradition), which determine capital requirements and financing transactions.
- Investing and financing have auxiliary functions to enable a firm's value creation process (mainly consisting of procurement, manufacturing, marketing)
- To ensure a financial equilibrium (i.e. short-term liquidity) is the main priority for financial management.
- Investment and finance are understood as stock and flow operations, that change the capital endowment of a firm.

Finance and investment understood as a descriptive science

- The academic focus is on taxonomies and financial contracts. Special references are given to the management of a firm's financial crisis.
- Cash flow financing and working capital management are of paramount importance.
- Strong ties exist with accounting and controlling (the treasurer`s view).

Fig. 2.2 Traditional corporate financial theory had a close link to business and the real sector

output—with the amount of capital input taken as fixed—the theory of financial management is expressly concerned with the relationship between profitability and the volume of capital used" (Solomon 1963, p. 12). In such a paradigm, *capital markets* in general were only of *minor importance*, also partly due to their nascent stages at the time.

After World War II, the needs of practitioners in finance dominated the research agendas of academics in the finance arena. The focus was on the managerial approach to finance, stressing the organizational requirements of planning and monitoring financial transactions inside a firm and the relationship with its share- and debtholders. The *treasury department* became the most important organizational home base of finance, responsible for the management of a firm's flow of funds and its capital structure. In large capitalized firms, the treasury department was headed or supervised by the controlling department. It developed new and powerful instruments for managing the flow of information and installing innovative planning and controlling tools and systems (Dauten 1948; Howard and Upton 1953). At the same time, the so-called decision approach of finance and investing emerged in order to rationalize investment decisions in firms. At first, the *focus* was again on *real investment projects* (Lutz and Lutz 1951; Dean 1951; Weston 1966). During the early post-World War II period, times were beginning to change as capital market theory emerged from the neoclassical paradigm of perfect markets, total equilibrium models, and contingent claims analysis.

2.1 The Building Blocks of the Modern House of Finance: Capital Market Theory and Finance

State-of-the-art finance and capital market theory as it exists nowadays in textbooks, academic thinking and practice is implicitly grounded on the assumption of a *monetary market economy*. Although financing processes such as saving and lending can be exercised in purely barter economies, the use of money eases economic transactions and reduces transaction costs (Alchian 1977; Hirshleifer 1973). In its research program *the microfoundation of money*, monetary theory constitutes the *three classical roles of money* in a market economy: as the means of exchange, the unit of account ("measure of value"), and store of value (Clower 1977). *Arrow*, *Debreu*, and *McKenzie* (ADM) demonstrated in their pioneering neoclassical total equilibrium models that the role of money has to be reduced to a *numéraire* (Arrow 1964; Debreu 1959; McKenzie 1959). It then can work like "grease" to facilitate frictionless economic transactions between agents and solve the *problem of double coincidence of wants*. For the allocations of goods and resources, the functioning of the pricing process, and the derivations of the equilibrium solutions in markets and the total economy, *money* is then *neutral*. In a complete and perfect market system of the ADM-type, money is *like a veil* and traded on a *residual market* (the money market) and is solely required to make the system of mathematical equations solvable.

With the *neutrality of money*, financial *intermediaries* like banks, insurance companies, etc. specialized in facilitating financial processes by the use of special monetary contracts are *superfluous*. As the later following work of, e.g., *Benston* and *Smith* (1976), *Diamond* (1984), *Greenbaum* et al. (1981), and others demonstrated, such financial middlemen are only needed in a capital market system if special *information asymmetries* and *agency problems* occur. As practice demonstrates, this is not an exception but in fact the rule, and therefore financial intermediaries play an important role for the functioning of a monetary and market economy alongside money and financial contracts.

The special role of money in neoclassical equilibrium models is much more fundamental, as it allows the *quantitative* and the *qualitative dichotomy of the total economic system* into two subsystems (Samuelson 1968, p. 3). The real sector encompasses the allocation and the price formation of nonmonetary goods. In the monetary sector (money and capital markets) and the microeconomic setting, the relative prices of financial contracts are fixed, and on a macroeconomic basis, the overall price level is determined. This describes the *quantitative dichotomy* (Modigliani 1963, pp. 83–84). From a technical point of view for modeling economic systems by mathematical equations, such a distinction seems appropriate as it eases the handling of the complexity, interaction, and interdependency of all components of an economic system (the so-called *Cournot* problem, Hoover 1984, pp. 64–65). However, the former sketched quantitative dichotomy worked well for economic modelings and equilibrium solutions and implicitly pervades financial models, e.g., option pricing models.

What is underestimated so far is the relevance of the *qualitative dichotomy*. To assume the neutrality of money might help for finding smart solutions that often help a lot in solving problems in daily economic life. On the other hand, operating in an environment of a quantitative dichotomy obscures the effects of money and the monetary sector on the allocation processes in the real sector. As the microeconomic-based monetary theory has proven (e.g., Brunner and Meltzer 1971; Alchian 1977), the introduction of money in a nonmonetary economy is justified by a welfare argument. Money ideally reduces transactions costs, eases economic transactions, avoids uncertainties in nonmonetary economies (e.g., the due to the problem of double coincidence of wants), and is a precondition for economic growth and welfare. With such a function, money and monetary contracts are neither neutral nor an isolated sector. Due to its *focal role* for the functioning of an economic system money, capital markets and financial intermediaries require a special attention (e.g., of regulators which define the rules and institutions for a workable financial system). However, the *qualitative dichotomy* in the neoclassical paradigm might *support* a *separated thinking* and *acting* in economic sectors which indeed are closely tied together. If such actually close ties loose, negative spillovers from the monetary and financial sector to the real sector might occur and disturb the efficiency of an entire economic system.

It is necessary to recapitulate the role of money, financial contracts, and financial markets to make aware of the implicit foundations of modern theories of capital markets and finance. They are based on the neoclassical total equilibrium paradigm and the related understanding of the role of money and financial contracts. A further summing up of the hidden neoclassical roots of modern finance leads to the *marginal utility school* (represented by *Carl Menger*) which will also be of significance in the following sections. Financial assets in the total equilibrium modeling have to be understood as coming from money-derived contracts that transform money over time (through the rate of interest) and handle risk. As derivatives of money, financial assets should also be neutral with reference to the equilibrium in a real market economy (see Fig. 2.3).

Finance theory and capital market theory can then be interpreted as a layer below the total equilibrium approach. They refer to the *microeconomic spheres*. Here most of the fundamental ideas refer to the early and groundbreaking works of *Irving Fisher* on interest rates and investment decision-making (Fisher 1930). *Fisher* could be understood as the predecessor of an equilibrium oriented, neoclassical-grounded capital market theory as it evolved in the late 1950s. In fact he implicitly operated in the manner of the neutral money paradigm by introducing of the separation and the value additivity theorem. Following on from there, investment decisions are made, *neglecting* the *financing conditions and individual utility functions* of agents. As today's textbooks state in nearly the same manner, the entire decision-making process for investments is then solely based on the *marginal productivity of capital* (i.e., the internal rate of return or marginal efficiency of capital) (e.g., Brealey et al. 2011). In addition, as *Fisher* explained: "The Principle of Maximum Present Value: Out of all options, that one is selected which has the maximum present value reckoned at the market rate of interest" (Fisher 1930, p.12). His sole *focus* on *cash*

Neoclassical (capital market driven) paradigm	
▪ **Separation theorem**: Liquidity risk of a firm depends on financial management, has to ensure the survival of the firm, and the profit risk is determined by a firm's procurement, production, marketing. ▪ **Corporate finance** is understood as a process of optimal participation in a firm's financial success: Net cash inflows of a firm's investment projects have to be distributed among capital providers according to their role as share- and debtholders.	**Type of financial contract matters:** ▪ Determined by the selected rule of future and uncertain cash flow distributions of financed investments (debt or equity or both). ▪ Future and uncertain cash inflows should be vested into such specific contracts so that they can be placed in the capital markets according to individual risk and return preferences of different types of investors. ▪ The sale of such contracts allows capital inflows into the firm.

Fig. 2.3 The neoclassical paradigm in financial theory—still alive

flows stemmed from the crucial assumption that investors' only economic driver is the maximization of their individual utility functions (to satisfy their "hunger for experience"; see Fisher 1930, pp. 10–12) by increasing monetary income outflows from investment projects. Needless to say, such a paradigm makes no obvious reference to ethics or morals. It is a *strictly hedonistic* understanding.

However, what makes the *Fisher's* assumption so relevant to ethical considerations are his (and his followers') *fundamental convictions*. In order to become a *respected science*, finance theory and capital market theory ought to lean on *natural sciences*, especially on physics. "In all of these areas (price formation, the monetary system, interest) Fisher proceeded by translating problems that had been understood in terms of differentiated social actors and goods into the terms of a mechanical system equilibrating a homogeneous substance" (Breslau 2003, p. 399). Under these circumstances, an intensive *analysis of utility functions* is *superfluous* as it is substituted by axiomatic conditions. "To fix the idea of utility the economist should go no farther than is serviceable in explaining economic facts. It is not his province to build a theory of psychology" (Fisher 1892, p. 11). *Fisher* refused to go any further into psychological, sociological, and even ethical foundations of utility functions. It was merely for the sake of being accepted as a well-respected scientist *keeping up with natural scientists*—as he stated very pronouncedly: "But the economist need not envelope his own science in the hazes of ethics, psychology, biology and metaphysics" (Fisher 1892, p. 23). This basic conviction spread among academics in the years following *Fisher's* statement and has lasted among the majority of capital market theorists until today, as we will see later on.[1]

[1] *Fisher's* point of view and self-understanding is very reminiscent of the later so-called *debate on positivism* that underwent an intensive programmatic discussion in economics under the umbrella of the monetarism debate between the two Nobel laureates *Milton Friedman* and *James Tobin.*

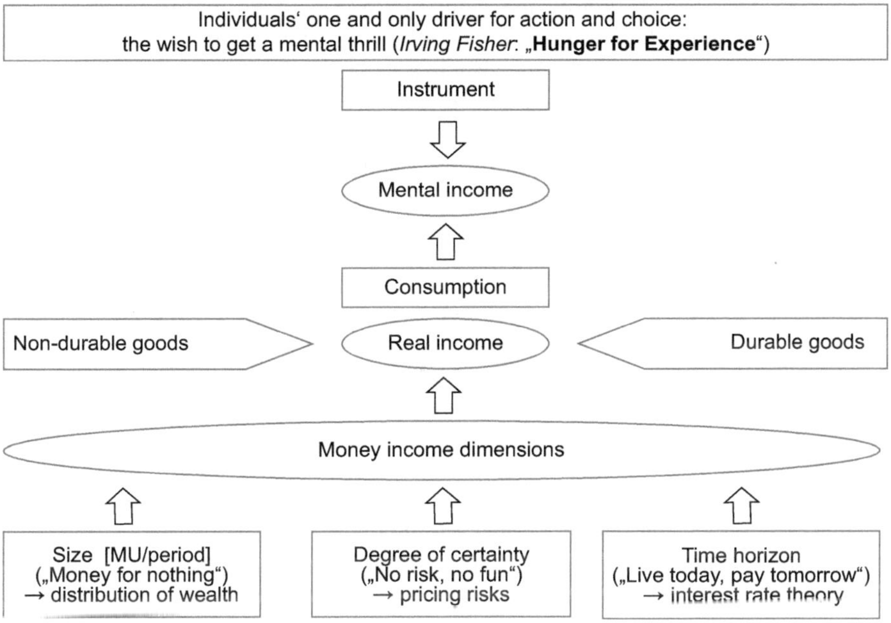

Fig. 2.4 The crucial role of *Irving Fisher* in finance theory: men's actions are driven by satisfying the appetite and permanent search for happiness

Fisher's fundamental point of view highlights the reasons responsible for ignoring individual utility functions and the differences between them with respect to the preferred money amount (amount preference), the degree of certainty (risk preference), and the date of availability (time preference) of cash flows. Utility as a very subjective term for the psychological state of individual agents hinders interpersonal comparisons in economic transactions. With the *substitution of utility by a market-priced cash flow* from investment opportunities, the measurement of utility is no longer required. Instead, *utility* is expressed by a *universal monetary value* and in terms of *monetary units*. Differences in individual utilities can be matched in principle by individual lending and borrowing transactions on perfect capital markets. A *risk-free interest rate* expresses the *time value of money* and the overall price for the allocation of capital and related financial income streams (Fisher 1930, pp. 130–147). From a very particular ethical point of view, namely, the Christian Church, *Fisher's* underlining of the interest rate as the crucial economic regulator of different time preferences was completely in opposition to the right of people to take interest per se. Figure 2.4 demonstrates the basic ideas of *Irving Fisher*'s concept.

Friedman defended the research community of positivism. He argued that sound research can be based solely on axiomatic grounds and the resulting explanations are valid although they have not been verified through prior realistic circumstances (Friedman 1953, p. 4). *Tobin* criticized *Friedman* and his proponents for causing the so-called "post hoc ergo propter hoc" problem, i.e., missing a causal model as the underlying rational for empirical validity (Tobin 1970).

Fisher's idea of substituting the individual and complex utility function and, implicitly, the individual values of monetary cash flows with monetary market values and prices, together with the principle of *separating finance and investment* transactions, had tremendous impacts on his successors in capital market theory. The following fundamental issues reflect *Fisher's* overwhelming contribution even for the current state of capital market theory—and its *resistance* to addressing the matters of *ethics and morality*. *Etzioni's* statement that the neoclassical understanding has no moral dimension seems obvious, as the following explanations will demonstrate (Etzioni 1991, p. 355):

- The *assumption of a perfect capital market* is one of the implicit cornerstones of *Fisher's* paradigm. It is remarkable that the initial idea to formulate a perfect capital market served as a model (the ADM total equilibrium models) but over the following decades gained *normative power*. The most crucial outcomes of such a paradigm were deregulations of capital markets in many industrialized countries at the beginning of the new millennium.
- By substituting the individual utility function with *a universal market-priced cash flow income stream*, it became possible to generalize investment decisions for individual investors, based on derived parameters such as the net present value or the internal rate of return. Investors who took additional parameters into account like for instance social or ecological ones or any other ingredients outside the setting of the capital market theory when making investment decisions would be condemned to earning a return below market returns or suffer from extraordinary risky positions.
- Nobody, operating as a *rational investor*, would voluntarily incur a loss by investing outside *Fisher's* basic principles. Investors should stick to the idea of man as a *homo oeconomicus*. This rational, selfish yet highly knowledgeable agent would not operate within his individual utility function but instead with monetary cash flow-based market values. Any ethical or moral considerations would be anachronistic to him. Deviations from the principle of the maximization of individual income streams, such as altruism, and of getting individual satisfaction by anything else than spending income for the consumption of goods would not be in line with *Fisher's* way of satisfying a person's hunger for experience.
- The *separation principle* and the independence of investments from financing conditions opened the door for huge innovations in marketable financial contracts and were escorted by immense research dynamics in capital market theory. And so the development *separating the financial and the real side of an economy* was laid—a shortcoming that peaked in the subprime and banking crises 2008 and which is in *sharp contrast* to the need for an *integration of the financial and real sides* of an economy.

Figure 2.5 repeats the basic components of the modern view of finance coming up from *Fisher's* basic ideas. His separation theorem was refined by enriching the investment decision process with additional components like tax shields and other *financial side effects*. It was up to *Modigliani* and *Miller* (MM) to prove that, under

Modern finance (in the tradition of *Irving Fisher*)
➢ Monetary view of the firm, i.e., it is a source to generate different types of income streams (dividends, interest, taxes, salaries etc.) for different stakeholder groups.
➢ Target of the firm: Maximizing its market value (in a narrow sense its shareholder value) as a prerequisite to fulfill the different income expectations of the stakeholder groups.
➢ Only monetary cash flows matter.
➢ Finance and investment are decision problems for shareholders and bondholders to optimize their individual income preferences (with respect to time, amount and risk preferences).
➢ Consumption preferences are the main sources that constitute differences in individual income preferences of investors.
➢ A perfect and complete world of capital markets is the most important ingredient of this paradigm as it allows the transformation of investors' individual and often different time preferences.

Fig. 2.5 Financial management according to the neoclassical approach

the assumption of perfect capital markets, financing and investment processes are separable from each other (Modigliani and Miller 1958). Again, individual utility functions were of no concern. Debt financing could enlarge the capacity of a firm to invest, prompting many financial institutions like private *equity investors* and *hedge funds* to take advantage of *Modigliani* and *Miller*'s academic insights. With the introduction of the *arbitrage equilibrium principle*, even an investor's risk preference became obsolete. At that time the separation theorem and the neutrality of money was also inspired by the work of *Markowitz* on *portfolio selection* (Markowitz 1952).

As mathematics and statistics became the dominating analytical methods in capital market theory-related research in the second part of the twentieth century, his work also marked a new stage in the progress of capital market theorists' efforts to keep up with natural sciences. Instructive is the following citation at *Markowitz'* defense of his doctoral thesis when his opponent, Noble laureate *Milton Friedman*, said: "Harry, I don't see anything wrong with the math here, but I have a problem. This isn't a dissertation in economics and we can't give you a Ph.D. in economics for a dissertation that's not economics" (Bernstein 1992, p. 60). However, with his dissertation *Markowitz* opened the door for a new generation of "quants" in finance and economics. The new economics tackled *uncertainty and risk* not as an intransparent and cloudy issue. By making future events and their consequences for economic transactions calculable and computable, they *unveiled* the curtain of *mystic* and *miracle* that surrounded uncertainty and future in economics for a long time (Bernstein 1996, p. 217).

Markowitz' work was the beginning of a research program that extended his basic ideas of a general equilibrium concept. Its most prominent outcome was the *capital asset pricing model (CAPM)* as *Sharpe* (1964), *Mossin* (1966), *Lintner* (1965), and *Ross* (1976), independently from each other, have all formulated it. Financial decisions under uncertainty were reduced to a smart model, based on assumptions about a generalized optimization behavior. *Individual utility functions* (preferences) again became *irrelevant* for asset valuation due to the separation and value additivity theorems: individual preferences were independent among agents, and a market-related valuation is assumed to be always possible. The structure of a portfolio of assets does not matter as *Tobin* proved in his *two-fund principle* (another kind of separation theorem) (Tobin 1958). And if the unique market portfolio is held among all agents, investment decisions are then independent from underlying individual decisions concerning consumption and investment (i.e., saving) and are also not influenced by finance decisions (i.e., the capital structure). In such thinking, the value of a risk-bearing *asset* is reduced to a *monetary value* and *independent* of the underlying individual utility function of the cash flow stream itself (not of the risk preference)—and *of any ethical values.*[2]

The ADM total equilibrium model delivered a very important ingredient for the extension of the *Fisherian* separation principle in cases of uncertainty. By introducing a particular *good*, described by its anticipated *state-dependent* future outcome, the so-called contingent claim, a complete set of spot and future markets could be designed in general equilibrium models. The money values of assets were then dependent on their *expected returns and related risks*. The method of evaluating the asset is grounded in the *theory of expected utility*. A restricted system purely based on financial terms and goals ties together the three *Fisherian* dimensions driving economic behavior in financial matters—amount and time preferences were completed by the risk preference in the individual utility function.

The introduction of such a *substantive uncertainty* results from an *incomplete information vector* and is the traditional view of the *axiomatic theory of choice under uncertainty.*[3] *Hirshleifer* and *Riley* (1979, pp. 1377–1379) defined decision-making under uncertainty as a problem of choice described by the following relationships:

- A set of future states of the environment $s = (1,2,\ldots,S)$
- A set of possible actions $a = (1,2,\ldots,A)$
- A set of consequences resulting from the interactions and states of the environment $c(a, s)$
- A preference scaling or utility function defined over consequences u(c)
- A probability distribution function θ(s) expressing the decision-maker's beliefs as to possible environmental states

---

[2]The development of new classes of mathematical formulated valuation models with exact solutions has fascinated practitioners in capital markets until recently. With such tools, every skilled agent was able to calculate asset prices with his pocket calculator and later on with Microsoft Excel program and other claculation software. More complex calculations were eased by preprogrammed spreadsheets that could be retrieved by the F9 button. In a heretical article in the *Financial Times*, such agents therefore have been called *F9 monkeys* (Tett 2005) as they rely solely on mathematical operations without any deeper understanding of assumptions and model causalities that lie behind.

[3]Uncertainty can have two origins: lack of information (which is substantive uncertainty) and limited cognitive capabilities of decision-makers to consistently pursue their objectives with given information (represented by procedural uncertainty) (Dosi and Egidi 1991, p. 145).

Within the concept of *substantive uncertainty*, certainty presumes a cognitively competent decision-maker having perfect knowledge of relevant future states of environment. A future environmental state occurring with certainty can be attributed by a probability of one. In contrast, the concept of risk is characterized by the attribution of different probabilities to all possible future environmental states. Risk in the *Knightian* sense (Knight 1921) presumes that the probability of each future environmental state can be described by an *objective probability distribution function*, which refers to a mathematical or statistical probability (Kyläheiko et al. 2002, p. 74). Under those circumstances, it is assumed that behavioral risks do not occur. *Systemic uncertainty*, *fat tails*, and other deviations from the bell-shaped normal distribution function of the *Gaussian* curve are *irrelevant* in these models (Bernstein 1996, p. 6).[4]

However, *decision-making under uncertainty* is tricky as nominal amounts of future cash flows are state dependent so that the timing and the degree of uncertainty of individual cash flows may differ among investments. It is at this point that a deeper understanding of the *concept of utility* becomes important. Utility is the perceived degree of *satisfied individual wants* and is therefore *intangible* (how, e.g., is the "mental income" in the *Fisherian* sense defined?). But if *Fisher* was right, we can only explain economic behavior by knowing each other's utilities and preferences independent of the good serving as a means of achieving "experience and happiness." Such a situation is best represented by a barter economy. But a pure barter economy burdens on economic transactions high (sometimes prohibitive) costs, markets reduce transaction costs, and money goes one step further: as financial assets stem from money-derived contracts to transform money over time (via the interest rate) and to handle risk with contingent claims, they extend the *money market* of the ADM model to the capital market.

Along with this approach, the valuation and comparison of uncertain future cash flows might differ between agents. The optimal link would be the *certainty equivalent* according to the individual's expected utility, which might be subjective following differences in individual agents' perceptions. Both shortcomings require a *common denominator* for state-dependent future cash flows evaluated to the present (i.e., discounting). As a simplified approach, the *monetary value* was introduced as a *proxy* for the *individual value in a utility function*. Moreover, inside such a function, the risk premium substitutes the individual certainty equivalent. The replacement is more than a technical matter. The substitute is established in (efficient) capital markets and represents a kind of a public good as it can be derived for every rational market participant with low transaction costs by studying the risk-adjusted asset prices in capital markets. Figure 2.6 illustrates the structure of such a causality.

The integration of uncertainty, risk aversion, diversification, market pricing of assets, ambitious assumptions of expectation formation, and the information efficiency of capital markets became crucial for what *Haugen* (1995) later on called *New*

[4]So-called Black Swans as *Taleb* (2007) has discussed it.

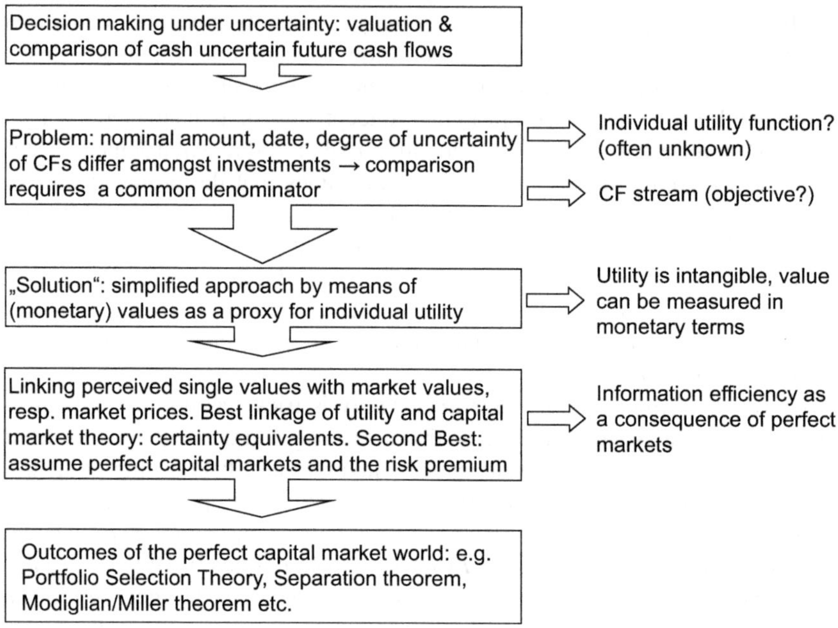

Fig. 2.6 Why capital markets matter in modern finance

Finance. Profit and related income maximization became the sole drivers for economic decisions and transactions. Economic agents were assumed to have homogenous and rational expectations.[5] As stated by the underlying *state preference theory*: "The individual subjective beliefs concerning the probabilities of the future state of nature" (Copeland et al. 2005, p. 103). Agents have access to objective information, i.e., information assumed to be complete, real-time, correct, costless, and public. The underlying *rational expectation hypothesis* (REH) and the *hypothesis of information-efficient* capital markets (MEH) allow agents *independent* and *rational behavior*. This stated the so-called *joint hypothesis*. It has, until today, also delivered the two fundamental pillars of modern capital market theory. According to *Fama's* work, it guarantees the *no-arbitrage principle* that has become the cornerstone of the *equilibrium paradigm in modern capital markets*, as, in the short term, rational speculators and arbitrageurs eliminate the failures of other market participants and hold the price formation process, more or less, at an equilibrium (Fama 1970, 1991). Individuals can make errors but sooner or later they are eliminated from capital markets according to the law of large numbers.

It was up to *Black*, *Scholes*, and *Merton* to extend the logic of probability theory in order to elicit the fair value of derivatives, namely, "options" (Black and Scholes 1973). The *Black/Scholes formula* demonstrated that spot market transactions and

[5]"Expectations, since they are informed predictions of future events, are essentially the same as the predictions of the relevant economic theory" (Muth 1961, p. 316).

the values of market traded financial contracts can be mobilized to evaluate derivatives if the no-arbitrage equilibrium principle holds. As previously, the work of *Markowitz*, *Sharpe*, *Ross*, and others had *encouraged asset managers* and the financial industry to design different asset allocation strategies and sophisticated financial products and to install investment styles, i.e., to deviate from a unique market portfolio as the CAPM has claimed for. The *Black/Scholes* formula and enhancements like the *Cox/Ross/Rubinstein* (Cox et al. 1979) model and others opened the door to a world of financial markets becoming more and more separated not only from real investments but from the real economy as a whole. With the *no-arbitrage equilibrium concept* that represents the cornerstone of most of the derivative valuation models, no recourse to the utility concept was necessary. With the emergence of a new school of highly sophisticated mathematicians and physicians with *Merton* at the spearhead and supported by the Noble laureate *Paul A. Samuelson*, the victory of the capital market paradigm with close ties to natural sciences had firmly taken place (Samuelson 1998). Firms and other economic entities listed on securities exchanges were solely evaluated by their financial performance expressed in monetary terms like dividends, stock prices, etc. In the sense of *Fisher*, *finance* now stood at the front door of the temple of natural sciences. *Financial chemistry* and *financial engineering* became the embodiments of a respectable financial science compared to natural sciences and engineering.

With the dominance of capital markets and their way to understand values, the management of faceless firms required the *delegation principle*, accompanied by rules of *corporate governance* in order to reduce *opportunistic behavior* of a firm's management and to avoid related *agency costs*. Ideal and efficient capital markets have to monitor such deviations from an equilibrium model, to set correct incentives to minimize agency costs, and to sanction poor-performing managers with the threat of unfriendly takeovers and the possible loss of their income sources (Jensen and Meckling 1976, p. 308). Increasingly with the neo-institutional economics, *uncertainty* was not only understood as an exogenous matter but could also be caused by the behavior of managers, investors, etc., i.e., could have an *endogenous* character and lead to *behavioral risks* (Alchian and Allen 1983, p. 184). Quality uncertainty, holdup, and moral hazard could occur and cause severe transaction costs. Inefficient market transactions, adverse selections, and a complete breakdown of markets could be the negative consequences. Figure 2.7 illustrates the different milestones in finance and capital market theory.

According to the dominance of the *neoclassical paradigm* of the theory of finance and capital market theory, agents, i.e. human beings, actually have no individual role to play. They are part of a game, and all behave in the same manner dictated by principles like rational expectation formation, income maximization, capital market efficiency, etc. Each agent is part of an exogenous process comparable to a *lottery* or game of roulette. *Price formation* processes of assets and investments are on a *random walk* expressed by statistics and mathematics like martingales and exogenous probability functions. The outcome of the game is independent of the mode of the formation and the distribution to each player, i.e., it underlies an exogenous stochastic process and is thus independent of an individual's market

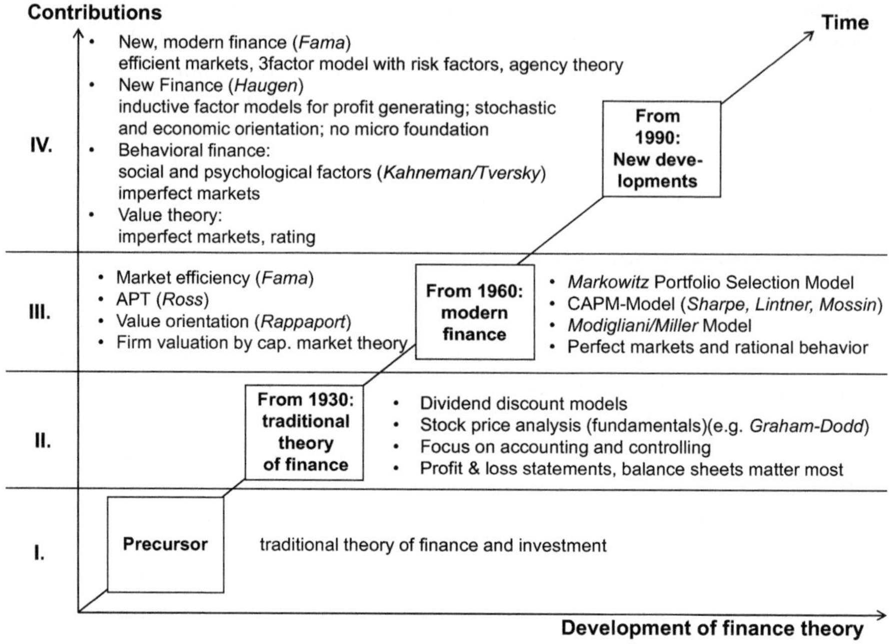

Fig. 2.7 Milestones in financial economics from a historical point of view

action (Shah 1997, p. 195). Under those circumstances, the *analogy to natural sciences*, e.g., biology and physics, becomes attractive. One of the most prominent adoptions is the *Brownian* motion and derived stochastic processes like the *Wiener* process to determine future asset price movements in modern valuation models: "Modern finance traditionally assumes that there is enough competition in markets that investors or firms can take prices as given and simply react to them. The fundamental work of Merton and Scholes is grounded in this assumption, as is virtually all subsequent research in derivatives pricing" (Stulz 2000, p. 7).

It was up to researchers and *Noble laureates* like *Shiller* (2003), *Kahneman* and *Tversky* (1979), and others who feel encouraged to risk research beyond mainstream capital market theorists. Those *challengers of the traditional neoclassical* capital market *theory* seemed to be inspired by the work of *Granger* and *Morgenstern*: "Ultimately a more descriptive work of the functioning of the stock market will have to be guided by psychological research, especially related to the psychology of crowds" (Granger and Morgenstern 1970, p. 22). Figure 2.8 contrasts the two different approaches in capital market theory.

One must confess that the proponents of *behavioral finance* are still not able to present a methodological closed paradigm that could challenge or substitute the neoclassical paradigm in capital market theory. However, their research has broadened the understanding of economic behavior on capital markets and financial transactions: *Heterogeneous investors* driven by various, sociodynamic motives,

Pillars of defenders

‚Modern capital market theory':

- Homogenous investors (profit/income maximization as the only driver for economic transactions)
- Perfect information (complete, real-time, correct, costless, polypolistic)
- Independent ‚rational' behavior (individual/collective)
- Individual failures match each other and are eliminated in markets according to the law of big numbers
- No-arbitrage principle as the corner-stone of an equilibrium in capital markets (rational speculators and arbitrageurs eliminate in the short run economic failures of other market participants, while on average the pricing process is in an equilibrium)

Statements of challengers

‚Behavioral Finance':

- Heterogenous investors (various, socio-dynamic motivations drive economic actions)
- Imperfect/incomplete information sets (information asymmetry/information diffusion matters)
- Behavior is dependant and often irrational (systematic anomalies of behavior)
- Misbehavior of individuals can lead to herdings and fails actions of individuals spill over to the whole market (via social imitation/social infection, herding etc.)
- Arbitrage processes are sub-optimal, conditions of no-arbitrage equilibrium concepts are violated, market participants behave irrationally

Fig. 2.8 The capital market paradigm is changing—and leaves space for new paths

often imperfect and with incomplete information, and limited knowledge of the state of the economic system can cause irrational behavior and suffer from bounded rationality. Such *anomalies* occur more often than capital market theory would expect and challenge the question whether such biases dominate the regular theory and make it less reliable.

Indeed, it seems that behavioral anomalies often become more or less *systematic*, mainly in times of turmoil. In addition, the impropriety of individuals can lead to social imitation and social infection wide-spreading the failures of some individuals through the entire capital market. *Arbitrage* processes then can become *suboptimal* and violate the conditions of the no-arbitrage equilibrium concept. "The behavior of financial markets is very much a social phenomenon. Peoples' decisions to buy, hold or sell securities are greatly influenced by what others are saying or doing" (Klausner 1984, p. 57). Although the school of behavioral finance makes many critical points challenging the robustness of the neoclassical capital market models, in fact it is in its core aiming to save the paradigm by setting complementary assumptions and axioms to existing models—which in fact can help to modernize them. However, the behavioral finance school left the door open when investigating the black box of human behavior and even their ethical attitudes and moral sentiments.

2.2 Crisis, What Crisis? The House of Finance in a Seismic Environment

Much hope was laid on the efficiency of capital markets in the outgoing twentieth century. Huge *deregulations* in many countries, the abolishment of the separating banking system mainly in the USA, the *digital revolution*, and the historically largest *worldwide integration of capital markets* were seen as the dominating drivers of an intensified research and development (R&D) in firms in the real sector, accompanied by an increase in the global trade of goods and services, which should lead to an overall growth in welfare.

Contrary to these expectations, there are many indications that, with the millennium, capital markets have operated in an *exuberant manner*. In many national economies, they lost their former strong ties to the real sector. They exacerbated problems in the world like controversies about soft commodity speculation and their impact on food shortages (e.g., the tortilla crisis), jeopardized price volatility, etc. On a macroeconomic level, voices raised that the ongoing *deregulation of markets* in total has created an *inequality* in many societies in favor of a small group of people who own and control the bulk of capital around the world (Stiglitz 2013; Picketty 2014; Atkinson 2015). Without deregulated capital markets, such a shift towards inequality would never be possible. In addition, another shape of capital market deregulation has developed: criminal activities with *huge financial losses* and *reputational damages*, e.g., SocGen's *Jérome Kerviel* (hazardous speculations, nearly 5 bn. USD loss for SocGen in 2001), *Bernard Madoff* (2008, cheats investors by about 1.4 bn. USD), Hedge Fund Manager *Raj Rajaratnam* (makes a profit about 66 m. USD with inside trading), UBS Trader *Kweku Adoboli* (2011, blows away 2 bn. USD), Deutsche Bank's Principal Trader *Christian Bittar*, and Barclays Bank's Trader *Philippe Moryoussef* (2018 manipulation of the EURIBOR at the height of the financial crisis).[6]

Besides the wrongdoing of individuals in the banking sector, the beginning of the second millennium decade has sounded the alarm about an organized criminal energy within banks as institutions. Apart from accusations of *fraudulent mispricing* in exchange rates in the currency markets or the criminal behavior in the fixing of reference money market rates like LIBOR or EURIBOR, several banks were convicted or have agreed to accept penalties. Such events reckon that especially investment banks have treated their counterparties unfairly and have run a system of false pricing for the benefit of a handful of financial intermediaries. Banks and banking have been increasingly accused of *unethical behavior* that can cause near-collapses of

[6]Sources: https://www.investopedia.com/articles/investing/020216/three-most-notorious-rogue-traders.asp; https://www.theguardian.com/business/2012/nov/20/ubs-rogue-trader-guilty-fraud; https://archives.fbi.gov/archives/newyork/press-eleases/2011/hedge-fund-billionaire-raj-rajaratnam-found-guilty-in-manhattan-federal-court-of-insider-trading-charges, https://www.sfo.gov.uk/2018/07/12/two-former-senior-bankers-convicted-of-fraud-in-sfos-euribor-manipulation-case/).

national economies and be a burden on societies due to severe welfare losses. The *subprime crises* at its spearhead urged an intensive discussion about the *power of banks* (*too interwoven to fail* argument) and how to regulate them. Such breaches of regulations intensified discussions about the need for a new understanding of morality and ethics in business practice—particularly in order to halt the *meltdown of* the *reputation* of the whole banking sector and the *erosion of* the *financial system* and to find a *new* understanding of the *relationship* between the *financial* (monetary) *and* the *real sector.*

Financial crises demonstrated among others that the link between the monetary, i.e., financial side and the real side of the economy, has become loose over time. It seems that separation and value additivity theorems have led to a private playing field in capital markets with agents much more engaged with betting against each other than feeling a sense of responsibility towards the real economy and society. *Money* has *changed* from *grease* and neutral numéraire *to* the *token* of a *gambling house*.

Unfortunately, the *gambling and their outcomes*, mainly asset prices, interest rates, and exchange rates, are linked to the real economy because they serve as signals for the allocation of capital, goods, and resources. Modern finance—in academia and in practice—has developed the contracts and valuation methods to make financial assets tradable but has increasingly ignored the anchoring to the real economy. Therefore, a renaissance in the purpose and the research programs of modern finance seems overdue. As *Zingales* (2000, p. 1624) pointed out: "The interaction between the nature of the firm and corporate finance issues has become so intimate that answering the fundamental questions in theory of the firm has become a precondition for any further advancement in corporate finance."

Closely related to an essential renaissance of corporate finance linked to the very nature of a firm is the current ongoing discussion about the *time horizon* of firm leaders and capital market participants. It is about the excessive focus frequently observed on *management short-termism*, *quarterly earnings*, and a corresponding *lack of* attention to *strategy*, *fundamentals*, *long-term value creation*, *corporate sustainability*, and *corporate social responsibility* (Dallas 2011, pp. 266–280). There is a widespread conviction that financial markets squeeze the management of public listed firms to act short-term minded. *Short-termism* is not restricted to the typical "quick win" seeking *hedge funds* and other aggressive investors (Brav et al. 2008). *Conventional investors* and *analysts* mostly face considerable short-term financial performance pressures from their clients and from the media. Moreover, even typical long-term investors as pension funds and foundations often appear, de facto, to be short-term minded. Short-termism is often criticized for the *inability of financial markets* to provide funds for long-term investments that deliver positive external effects like infrastructure projects, social investments, and measures that allow mitigating and adopting climate change (EU High-Level Expert Group 2018, p. 9).[7]

Positive external effects of finance and investment are in general attributed to sustainable and socially responsible investments. As they represent ethical considerations in economic activities, a *link* can be made that combines *time horizon*, *uncertainty*, and *ethics*:

- *The time horizons* of financial market participants can deviate from a *social time horizon* needed for long-term investments that contribute to social welfare. Short-termism is thus often *inconsistent* with a sustainability development approach and *biases the time value of money of related long-term investments*: The rate of return demanded by financial markets can be too high compared to the required lower *social interest rate* (i.e., the social discount rate) that characterizes many sustainable investments, i.e., infrastructure projects (Marglin 1963). This in turn can lead to negative net present values or low internal rate of returns. In such cases, private funding for long-term, socially relevant investments are not forthcoming, and private capital is unable to contribute to sustainable development (Henley and Spash 1993, p. 130).
- However, time inconsistencies might also arise due to an increased *uncertainty*. In times of highly volatile or turbulent environments in which financial market participants and firm managers have to make decisions, the shortening of the payback period for investment projects might serve as a kind of risk reduction. If such circumstances frequently occur, private investments in firms and financial markets would exhibit biases toward short-termism. Such trends may accelerate, if the regulatory environment proves unreliable, creating regulatory uncertainty, which often happens with regard to environmental and social issues.
- Since 2015, and inspired by the Paris agreement on climate change (*COP 21*), public institutions (e.g., G20 Green Finance Study Group 2016) and many national governments have prompted the private financial sector to mobilize private capital. The ultimate goal is to finance urgently needed investments that can cope with the negative consequences of climate change and can reduce the negative contributions of production and consumption to global warming (World Bank 2012). The fight against the causes of *global warming* and the attainment of the *Sustainable Development Goals* (OECD 2016) demonstrate the vital need for a comprehension of and challenges to the current sustainable development approach. Sustainable investments are increasingly understood as pivotal for the transition to a sustainable economy in general and to a greenhouse gas-reduced environment in particular. "Long-termism describes the practice of making decisions that have long-term objectives or consequences. Investments into environmental and social objectives require a long-term orientation" (European Commission 2018, p. 4).

---

[7]Similar arguments can be found in publications of supranational organizations, e.g., UNEP (2015), UNCTAD (2015), UNEP FI (2018), and United Nations Framework Convention on Climate Change (UNFCCC) (2010).

The explicit consideration of the elements within the *theory of firms* and the *link between time, risk, and ethics* became relevant in a newly emerging field called *sustainable finance*, in which all types of stakeholders (and not only share- and debtholders) have important roles to play for the allocation of capital (Soppe 2004).[8]

2.3 Rigor Versus Relevance: The Potential of Sustainability to Promote a Scientific Revolution Program in Finance in the Sense of *Kuhn*

With the ongoing debates and discussions about the relationship between finance and ethics, *corporate social responsibility* (CSR), the *concept of sustainable development*, and the roles of *stakeholders*, questions have been raised as to whether the current understanding of finance and capital markets is on the eve of a new paradigm. It would be a too extreme position to argue that a rapid change in the dominating paradigms of how firms operate, markets function, etc. might occur in the near future. As *Kuhn* (1970, pp. 10–23) worked out, science should be understood as *shifts of scientific programs*. A paradigm shift accompanies each change in such a program. *Kuhn* identified the logic of such a process as described in Fig. 2.9.

It would be exaggerated to state that economics as a science in general, and capital market theory in particular, together with corporate finance, are undergoing a concrete scientific revolution. However, one cannot ignore the fact that many of the pillars of the past's groundbreaking models like the CAPM or the MM theorem experience permanent critics from practice and from science. *Business ethics* can here play a prominent role. In the following, two examples will describe confrontations between conventional and ethics-related subjects of finance.

2.3.1 Stakeholder Versus Shareholder

As pointed out in the preceding chapters, shareholders as well as debtholders deserve essential rights in finance and capital markets owing to their special capacity for providing firms with funds. The availability of capital and liquidity is crucial to any firm's survival and growth. It is the main input factor for a firm's value creation. Moreover, *shareholders* are *owners of property rights*, which give them several entitlements to monitor a management's actions, to sanction it, and to influence business strategy. In traditional capital market theory and the theory of finance, *shareholders* used to be considered as *rational* agents with solely financial goals. This is part of the notion that a capitalistic system is based on property rights in the hands of private agents. Due to this legal prerequisite and the capacity of

[8]Stakeholders are "(...) those groups who can affect or are affected" (Freeman 1984, p. 49).

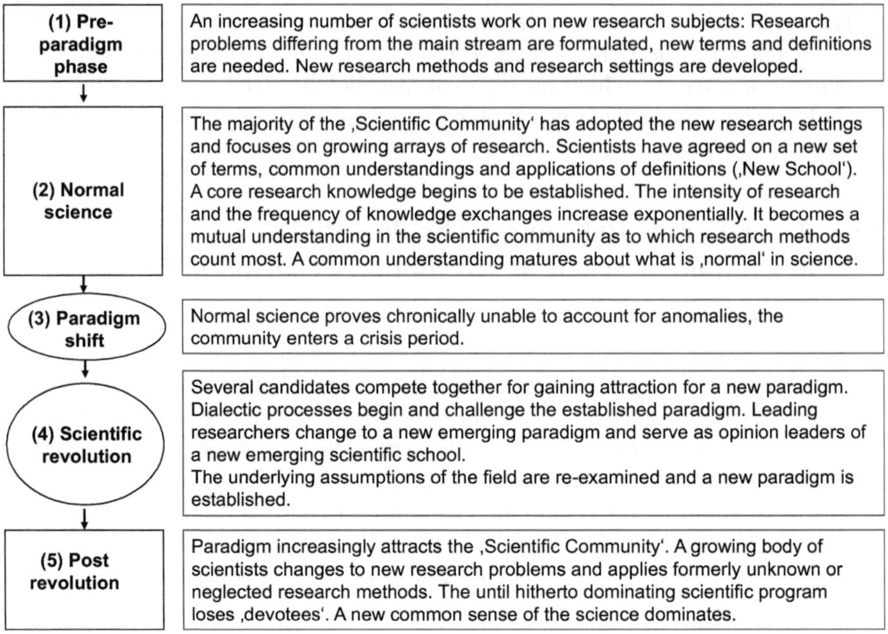

Fig. 2.9 *Kuhn's* model of scientific revolutions

shareholders to *reduce agency costs*, they are the dominating stakeholders, followed by debtholders as both are lubricating economic transactions with monetary funds. Capital market models are then ruled by the strict quantitative trade-off between expected return and risk.

These models are judged as *ethics free*. Moral problems implicitly refer to a fairness principle (sometimes game): agents maximize their utility, etc. A *causal link* between *fairness*, *operational efficiency*, and *financial goal* setting is often denied. Corporate governance research delegates ownership-related subjects and their inherent influence on economic productivity to other scientific disciplines. In an ideal sense, firm control is a matter solely for markets and the operations taking place there to sanction a management (e.g., by unfriendly takeover transactions).

Contrary to that position, it is evident that conflicts of interests between two groups frequently occur: shareholders' goal is to maximize their private monetary income, e.g., by dividend payouts, the remaining (nonfinancial) stakeholders often have to pay the price (e.g., fired workers, customers facing low product quality, communities affected by waste pollution, etc.).

Under these circumstances profit maximization causes *negative external costs* when, for instance, jobs were lost, taxes not paid, etc. In the past, a strictly shareholder orientation often has led to controversies between shareholders and remaining stakeholders. Not seldom, market-based distributions of income and wealth were criticized by stakeholders and by society at a whole as *unsocial or unfair*. Other negative external effects like the extensive business activities with massive adverse public effects (e.g., advertisement) often affect many parts of daily life and conquer the mind-sets of people. *Klein* (2000) complains that the focus on money and economics has led to its domination in each corner of daily life and has *reduced freedom and individual self-determination*. Related questions and occasional conflicts allude to subjects that are strongly related to business ethics and morality. Meanwhile a growing body of managers from firms operating globally accept that such externalities exist and are willing to enter into dialogues, for instance, with NGOs.

2.3.2 The Paradox of Social Costs

Another field of neglected interactions between ethics and economics is the paradox of social costs. The *neoclassical paradigm* emphasizes topics like operational efficiency, allocation optimization, and the maximization of shareholder value. Managers ought to act as agents for shareholders and have no mandate to embark on socially responsible projects that do not enhance the income generating potential of firms. As *Friedman* stated: "The only responsibility of a corporation is to deliver a profit to its shareholders" (Friedman 1970). Governments have to set the rules as what managers are permitted to do. Everything that law does not forbid seems allowed, even if it is questionable whether it is actually legal from a moral point of view (*legitimacy*). This conviction in the eyes of many market participants and not to underestimate the views of politicians bears the risk that market outcomes become deformed and the *invisible hand in markets* (as *Adam Smith* pointed out) suffers from a severe shock when markets end in crisis.

The *social contract theory* as a partial counterpart to the neoclassical purely economic theory uses a broader definition of agency relations. Not only shareholders but also *society* can be interpreted as the *principals of managers* (Cornell and Shapiro 1987). It is interesting now to admit that, under certain circumstances, the stated increase of a firm's overall costs when it internalizes negative external effects can avoid adverse effects on its financial key performance indicators and on shareholders' wealth. *Pava* and *Krausz* (1996) proved as one of the first that the existence of firm costs resulting from voluntary social and/or environmental activities does not automatically lead to an inferior financial performance of a firm, as standard capital market theory and corporate finance maintain.

From a more dynamic point of view and more than ever in a globalized economy, *NGOs* claim to *represent eligible interests of single groups of stakeholders* or parts of society. They threaten firms with *activism* that could harm a firm's reputation followed by adverse effects on their financial performance. Beyond any national *laws to operate*, which can only be partly enforced in a globalized world and therefore offers firms many ways of shirking, NGOs bargain with firms about their *license to operate* (see in details Sect. 5.2). A firm fulfilling the demands of NGOs, generally speaking to internalize negative external effects of environmental pollution, initially operates with a worsened cost function but later regains stability and reliability for its own value creation process. Under these circumstances, *shareholders' time preferences* should be more medium- or long-term. On the other hand, the benefits of a collaboration with NGOs are sometimes hazardous, and the positive financial outcome might be random. Nevertheless, surveys repeatedly reveal that many firms' managements accept that NGOs contribute most to advance sustainability issues (e.g., GLOBESCAN 2017, p. 9).

Chapter 3
On Values: The (Hidden) Ethical Framework in Capital Market Theory (An Outline of Ethics in Economics and Finance)

Abstract Beyond a very dominant reluctance among many practitioners and academics in finance and capital markets to accept the relevance of ethics and morality, a closer look behind the curtain of the technically minded understanding of financial modelling reveals interesting links between finance and ethics. Starting with a more religious observation concerning finance and its rivalry with economics, an introduction to basic elements of ethics is being presented here. It can be clearly demonstrated that virtue, deontological, and teleological ethics can contribute to financial matters but have fallen into oblivion over the last century. Of greatest concern is the role of utilitarianism as part of teleological ethics as it implicitly underlies the neoclassical-based finance and capital market theory. Also the unveiling of the hidden ethical roots of finance and capital markets, exemplary contributions demonstrate how the gap between ethics and finance could be bridged.

Keywords Virtue ethics · Deontological ethics · Teleological ethics · Religion · Separation principle · Financial market efficiency · Rational expectations · Interest rate

Modern finance and capital market theories reduce the complexity of finance and investment processes, the interactions of agents, the setting of rules, and, at the very least, the entire financial value creation process down to *mathematical and statistical operations*. Human behavior is simplified into only following the assumptions and axioms for an optimal allocation in capital markets. As strictly rational agents, who exploit all available information in markets, their daily bread is simply to optimize their individual wealth positions. According to the *neoclassical paradigm*, a human being (an agent) actually has no character as an individual personality. Economic agents are part of a well-defined system of complete, perfect capital markets and are assumed to behave as such (forming rational and homogenous expectations, maximizing their wealth or income, etc.). The outcome of market transactions is based on an arbitrage and (ethically) value-free equilibrium process. Under those circumstances, it seems obvious that *modern finance and capital market theory* is *free of*

H. Schäfer, *On Values in Finance and Ethics*, SpringerBriefs in Finance,
https://doi.org/10.1007/978-3-030-04684-2_3

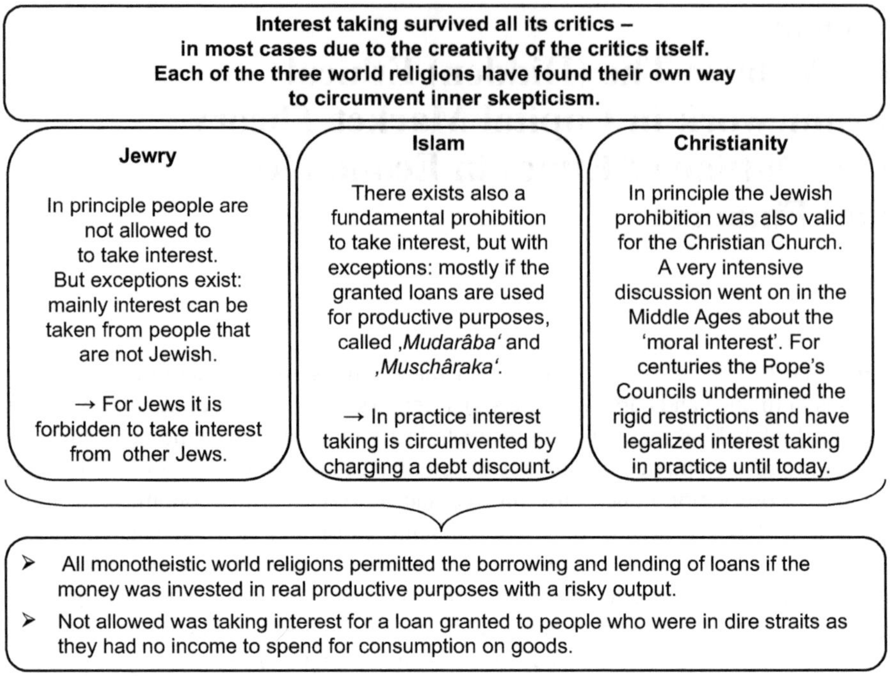

Fig. 3.1 Interest taking from the point of view of the world religions

ethical or moral values, and agents are operating according to quasi-laws of nature (Raines and Leathers 1994).

3.1 The Classical Links Between Values, Money, and Finance: Religions and Institutions

A new understanding of finance as a discipline with an ethical or moral background partly adheres to experiences stemming from the many controversies they faced in previous centuries among different world religions. Generally speaking, it is acknowledged that a certain type of *rivalry* has existed over the past centuries. This rivalry was between the *positive welfare effects of the use of money* and the practice of finance and the *negative impacts on people's welfare*. Figure 3.1 gives an overview of the partly overlapping positions of the Jewry, Islam, and Christianity concerning some basic positions about interest taking.

An unequal distribution of wealth between individuals was often justified by money's significant role in serving as an accelerator of envy, greed, or parsimony. From the point of view of a numismatist, it is interesting to learn that in the past two different symbols were very frequently embossed on each side of a coin, which is distinctly reminiscent of ***Aristotle's*** *distinction* of the usage of money—*oikonomia* and *chrematistics* (see Sect. 3.2.2)[1]:

- One side of the coin embodies the *bright side of money*. It reflects the capability of money to serve as means of exchange, unit of account, and store of value (see Sect. 2.1). Such functions could reduce the purpose of the usage of money to the following economic transaction chain: *goods → money → goods*. The embossed *head of the regent* who has issued the coin often expressed such a positive welfare economic function of money.
- The other side of the coin shows its *dark side*. Money is seen as a threat to individuals as it allows the conquest and subsequently the regulation of the minds, behaviors, and attitudes of people. In this case, the line of thought would be *money → goods → money*. To remind people of the dark side of money when using it in their daily lives, the reverse side of the coin was often embossed with a religious relic, mostly a *crucifix*, complemented by a citation. It represented a *warning sign*.

From a historic point of view, the relationship between money, resp., finance and religion, was determined by the big *controversies about interest* taking. Figure 3.1 gives an overview of the Jewish, Islamic, and Christian points of view concerning the legitimation of interest taking.

Some very fundamental *questions about money and ethics* were topics repeatedly brought up over past centuries. One of them was the question as to whether humans are allowed to take *interest*, i.e., the idea that demanding a value for time is a violation of the *privilege of God* who has the monopoly about time. If the latter were true, then *interest* taking by men would be a severe *sin*. Related to that question is the one that expresses doubts about the *fairness of taking interest* from a debtor. Is it fair to exploit someone's troubled economic situation by burdening him with the obligation of paying interest? Is the burden to repay the debt not in itself a burden that a debtor has to carry? No wonder that interest taking was traditionally banned by the *Catholic Church*, if interest was demanded for loans that were not invested in risky ventures or if the interest rate lay above an unethically high hurdle rate (the so-called *usurious interest* with a hurdle rate of more than *five percent* annually).[2] In other words, no prohibition was necessary if the *interest rate* was a *compensation for* the takeover of *risk*, e.g., the capital lender bears a risk with an investment he had financed through the loan. Moreover, it was self-evident that an interest rate below five percent was in line with the Catholic Church's position (see also Fig. 3.2 for a summary).

Despite the *official ban*, in practice, *interest taking spread* over time. Partly due to practical problems in implementing an effective ban on interest taking, it was more

[1] *Sedlacek* (2011) in general has elaborated a very sophisticated and fundamental discussion of the different strands of religious sources and drivers of economics.

[2] The ban of usury interest taking for Christians was proclaimed on the Nicene Council in the year 325 (Ballestero et al. 2015, p. 8).

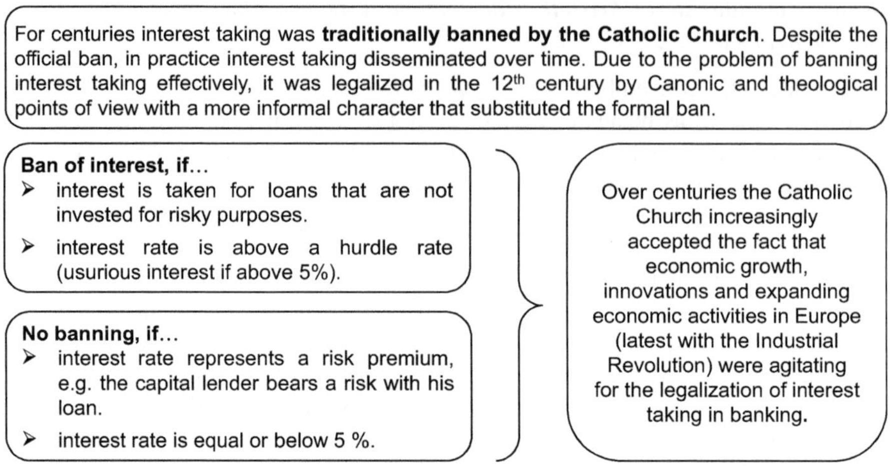

Fig. 3.2 Interest taking as a century-old controversy—the Catholic Church's point of view

or less legalized in the twelfth century. The formal ban was substituted by canonic and theological points of views of a more informal character. For centuries the Catholic Church increasingly accepted that economic progress in Europe (at the latest with the Industrial Revolution), and added pressure to legalizing the practice of interest taking in banking with the *Codex Iuris Canonic* (CIC) number 1543 in the year 1918. Although in monotheistic religions differing reasoning for the ban of interest taking existed, there is one common denominator. In principle, they all *accepted interest taking* if it was a *compensation for productive risky investments financed by loans*. The justification of an interest rate as a compensation for risk bearing is obvious. It is worth noting that such a grounding of the interest rate cannot be found in the state-of-the-art interest rate theories like the time preference theory of *Irving Fisher* and *Eugen Böhm von Bawerk*, the classical/neoclassical theories of interest, the *Keynesian* liquidity preference theory, or the theory of natural interest of *Knut Wicksell* just to mention a few prominent representatives of theories of interest.

The transition of the Catholic Church's restrictive attitude towards interest taking and other religious motives have survived until today and have had a strong influence on how capital markets and finance should be judged from an ethical point of view. The emergence of *socially responsible investments* (SRI) would not be possible without the initiatives and the persistence of investors from Churches and religious faith communities. Figure 3.3 gives an idea of some of the most important benchmarks in SRI, indicated by investment products that have been launched in the past. *Islam* and *Sharia Law* has given another strong religious impetus to financial markets (Siddiq 1995). Today the so-called *Islamic Finance* movement is popular not only in Islamic countries but also beyond. In countries like the United Kingdom (UK), it has established a fast-growing industry with asset management and financing guidelines that to some degree differ from mainstream capital markets (Errico and Farahbaksh 1998, pp. 6–11).

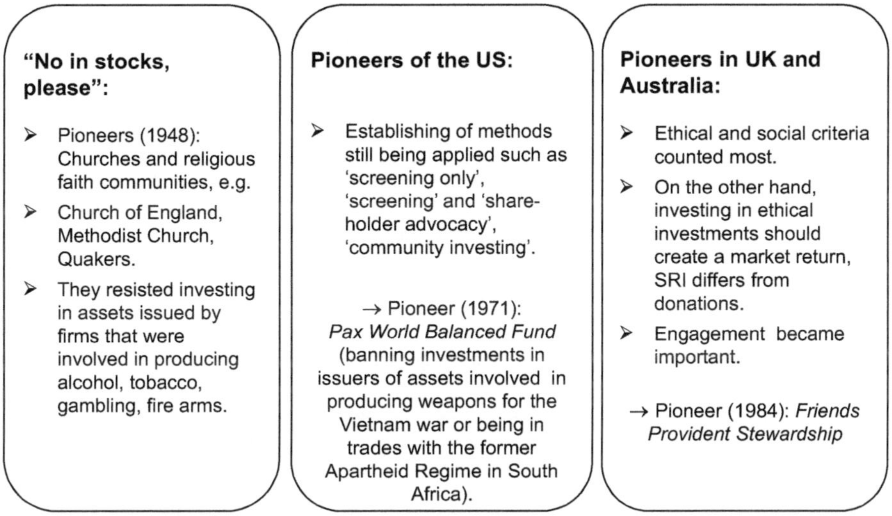

Fig. 3.3 A view into the present: socially responsible investments were first known as "ethical investments"

3.2 Ethics and Finance: The Matrix

As argued in Sect. 2.1, the conventional theory of finance and capital market theory rely on the separation theorem as well as the concept that monetary cash flow streams evaluated in perfect capital markets nowadays need greater psychological, sociological, and ethical considerations. At first glance, capital market theory and the resultant behavior of market participants seem to operate in an *ethical vacuum*.[3] The following demonstrations will shed light on the hidden ethical blueprint of conventional capital market theory (see also Fig. 3.4). Before being elaborated, a brief introduction into ethics and morality will be given.

Ethics is generally understood as the study of principles or standards of human conduct, while *morals* mean socially accepted standards and fairness (Soppe 2000, p. 15). Ethics is also about the rational of moral principles and duties and is often confused with morality. The latter expresses that an agent is following universally accepted ethical norms in his social activities. *Morality* is therefore the system of values existing in a society. Using a frequently employed philosophical framework in business ethics, in the following we adhere to the *classical triad* of *teleological*,

[3]In some parts, this impression is due to the currently dominating self-understanding of economics as a science that is free of value judgements. This attitude also represents the outcome of a long tradition in the dispute over method in science between the *Austrian marginal utility school* represented by *Carl Menger* (White 2008) and the *historical-ethical school* represented by *Gustav von Schmoller* at the end of the nineteenth century (Shionoya 2001).

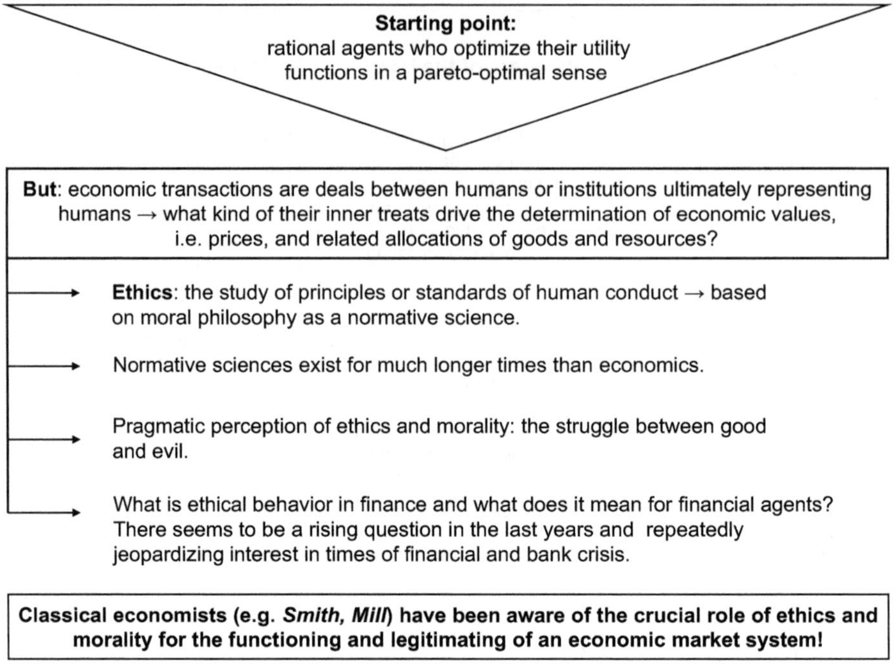

Fig. 3.4 Ethics as a benchmark for finance

virtue, and *deontological ethics* (Donaldson and Werhane 1996). Figure 3.5 outlines the different dimensions of these paradigms in ethics:

- *Virtue ethics* encompasses all ethics that are not based on moral laws, rules, or principles. The focus is on individual virtues and on inner traits, dispositions, and motives. Representatives of virtue ethics are among others *Aristotle*, *Plato*, *Smith*, *Marx*, and *Rawls.*
- *The deontological approach* underlines *duty* rather than virtue as the fundamental moral category. *One of the most important* representatives is *Immanuel Kant* with his *Kantian categorical imperatives* and his *principle of universalizability*: if somebody states that an activity is right for one person, then it follows that we are committed to a state that it is right for all other persons in similar situations. According to *Kant*, what count most for the ethical position of an individual are their *innate rights*, i.e., everyone's natural rights, which are independent of any juridical act and are consistent with a similar freedom for all people (Kant 1785). A modern representative of the deontological approach is *Sen* whose position will be explained in Sect. 3.2.2.
- *Ethics in the sense of the teleological approach* judges actions primarily with regard to the consequences instead of the acts themselves: human behavior is assumed to be *rational. Bentham and Mill* are the most prominent and classical representatives, and their influence will be clarified in the following:

Four constituting elements for an ethical framework following from philosophical discussion and research programs:

(1) motive of human activity, (2) human decision making, (3) instrument for wealth distribution, (4) moral responsibility

	Motive of human acting	Human decision making	Instrument for wealth distribution	Moral responsibility
VIRTUES, i.e. voluntary guidelines	inner freedom	intuition, metaphysics	ideological community thinking	individual
DUTIES, i.e. compelled goodness	external duties	social willpower	legal supervision	individual and collective
TELOS, i.e. rational goodness	consequences, goals	rationality	utility function	collective

Fig. 3.5 Overview of the ethical framework in finance (Soppe 2000, p. 24)

3.2.1 Building Blocks of Ethics with Respect to Economics and Finance

Although it is not usual to elaborate on ethics within finance, it is an implicit component, as many basic pillars of finance and capital market theories are based on the neoclassical paradigm (Sen 1987). Here the assumption of the rationality of a human being is a core element, embodied in the metaphor of the *homo economicus*. This ethical grounding is based on the notion of *utilitarianism* as *Bentham* and later *Mill* have formulated (Bentham 1789; Mill 1863). Their approaches belong to the category of teleological ethics and can be understood as *rational goodness*. They focus on the link between *actions and consequences* related to specific goals. Actions are primarily judged with regard to their *outcomes* instead of the basis of the actions themselves. In this sense, human behavior is assumed rational (Baron et al. 1997, p. 151).

This approach links the intended actions of capital market participants with their outcomes, like stock price movements, reallocations of asset portfolios, etc. The ethical value of capital market transactions will be judged by society's contentment generated by the initial actions of individual capital market participants. Each individual action would be ethically acceptable if the resulting sum of utilities or the average utility for a society have been increased.

According to *Bentham*, the principle of utility serves as the kernel, as actions are ethically and morally correct if their outcomes create the *greatest happiness for the greatest number of people* (Bentham 1789). Happiness is a hedonistic calculus and equivalent to pleasure. This image of happiness fits with *Fisher's* notion of "hunger for experience" that ultimately drives agents when they invest in ventures. Future cash flows from a venture generate monetary income, which enables an agent to consume goods and to satisfy his hunger for experience (Fisher 1930, pp. 10–12). If a mathematical calculation of such an economic *concept of happiness and pain* was possible, a teleologist would be able to state what was right and what was wrong. In *Fisher's* sense, one could argue that the calculated present value of a future cash flow from an investment project creates the monetary income for an investor and allows him to spend on the consumption of goods that deliver happiness in his individual utility function. If everyone behaved and calculated in this way, the happiness of the entire society can be maximized.

Mill extended *Bentham's* concept in his work "utilitarianism" to the idea that people may *differ* in the *quality* of their *pleasure* (Mill 1863; Boatright 1999, p. 36). The question would then arise as to how individually different utilities should be expressed and calculated. As argued in the previous sections, *Fisher's* solution was a universal substitute for individual utility with general monetary and market-priced economic values. Years later and with the upcoming of neoclassical mathematical and statistical valuation and risk models, *utilitarianism* became an implicitly integral part of modern capital market theory. However, utilitarianism as the core ethical basis of utility functions and rational decision-making in the face of risk and uncertainty was almost hardly expressed in all of the well-known valuation models like CAPM, APT, etc. Therefore it is remarkable, what one of the most prominent representatives of modern quantitative capital market models, *Markowitz*, in an interview given in 2016 uttered with respect to implicit utilitarianism in his models: "(...), if you maximize the expected value of one, you must approximately maximize the expected value of the other" (Kritzman and Markowitz 2017, p. 19). *Teleological ethics* is quite different from virtue ethics, which encompasses all ethical attitudes that are not based on moral laws, rules, or principles. The focus of virtue ethicists is on individual *inner traits*, *dispositions*, and *motives*. Representatives are ancient Greeks, mainly *Aristotle* and *Plato*.

The third school of ethics is represented by *deontological ethics*. Here, duty rather than virtue is the fundamental category, and it is often associated with the *Kantian* categorical imperative. *Sen* and partly *Rawls* are modern representatives of this school (Sen 1987; Rawls 1971). Although the dominant role of teleological ethics for the neoclassical paradigm and capital market theories is obvious, *Baron* et al. argued that there is enough space for the integration of the remaining two categories (Baron et al. 1997, p. 151).

3.2.2 Ethics in the Neoclassical Paradigm and in the Theory of Finance

It is worth noting that the normative science to which ethics belongs to has existed much longer than economic science. The separation of economics and ethics, as we

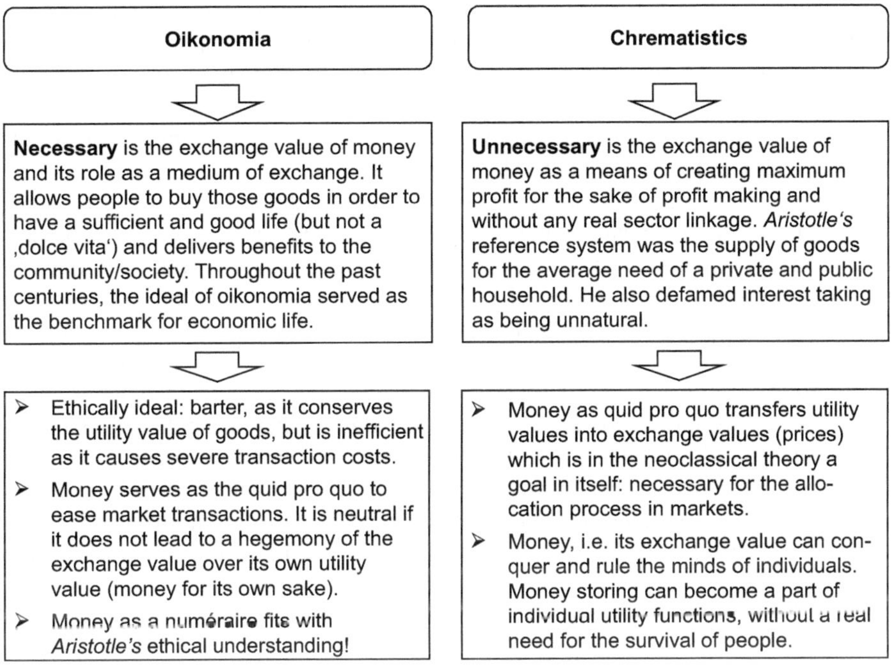

Fig. 3.6 *Aristotle*: economic value separated into use value and exchange value

perceive it today, is, historically, considered to be still in its infancy. Two thousand four hundred years ago, it was *Aristotle* who distinguished between economics, ethics, and politics in his *pragmatic philosophy* but who did not separate them (see Fig. 3.6). In his famous distinction between *oikonomia* and *chrematistics*, he indirectly underlined that the use of money as a medium of exchange allows people to buy goods that permit them an adequate lifestyle. By doing so, individuals also do well in society as a whole. *Aristotle* criticized the use of money, when it was reduced to an instrument of creating a maximum of profit for the sake of profit making and without any real sector linkage (*chrematistics*), as one would say today. *Aristotle's* reference system was the supply of goods for the average need of a household. He also condemned interest taking as unnatural, and his implicit understanding was of *neutral money* (Bartlett and Collins 2011). His notion is similar to the neoclassical conception of money.

Strongly linked to *Aristotle's* dichotomy was his term of a fair (market) price (pretium iustum), a concept that for two centuries dominated the way that the problem of *fair price determination* was discussed. Following *Aristotle*'s fundamental work, the *Scholars of the Middle Ages* understood the concept of fair prices as follows: fair prices are those which clear markets by balancing supply and demand and determine the income that allows manufacturers to make their living. In financial matters, the fair price paradigm changed somewhat as it was related to interest rates.

For centuries, this was associated with notions that *interest taking is usury* (see Sect. 3.1) and should be restricted or even prohibited. The fair price approach was also a matter of *fairness between contract partners*. In his two pillars of justice, *Aristotle* distinguished between the *justice of exchange* (iustitia commutativa) which is a necessary basis for a fair price and *distributional justice* that encompasses distribution of wealth and income (iustitia distributiva) (Friedman 1987).

The paradigm of *oikonomia* implicitly determined the way that economics worked in Europe for many centuries: the manageable, need-oriented, and patriarchal economy of a household. The *focus* was *on justice*—in economic activities and the resulting prices. The *Scholars* divided *Aristotle's* concept into three separate but inwardly linked areas called *trivium*: ethics, politics, and economics. It is remarkable that efficiency as the cornerstone of modern economic thinking was not of the utmost concern to *Aristotle* and his followers.

Efficiency became a *dominant role* in economics after the publication of the fundamental work of *Smith's The Wealth of Nations* (Smith 1776). It is common to interpret his concept of a decentralized market economy with an *invisible hand* as a metaphor for a privately organized, nonregulated, and decentralized economic allocation process. In it, rational individuals solely maximize their own utility and ensure the optimal allocation of resources and goods. In his *The Wealth of Nations*, *Smith* indeed relegated the concept of *justice* to the fringe by focusing on the creation of *welfare* for a society through *economic efficiency*.

What is often disregarded in common perception is *Smith's* strong ethical background. He was very much adhered to the premises of the ancient *Greek Stoics* of whom *Aristotle* was one. Their belief was that human life should act in accordance with nature. In his work *The Theory of Moral Sentiments*, *Smith* emphasized the importance of ethics for the functioning of a market economy and that the invisible hand needed to be *twinned* by the *invisible morality* (Soppe 2000, p. 7). Contrary to many prevailing interpretations, *Smith's* market concept is not reduced to the homo economicus as a utility-maximizing, selfish, and rational individual. *Bassiry* and *Jones* (1993) emphasized that *Smith* also states that an individual can gain utility if he strives for altruistic behavior. The motivation of his economic activities is not limited to the maximization of income and the sole consumption of goods—as *Fisher* stated.

Despite the long tradition of ethical philosophers and ethically influenced classical economists, mainstream economic paradigms have been developed in the post-*Smithsonian*, i.e., neoclassical era, more or less without any explicit reflection of their ethical positions. The *paradigm of economic efficiency* had crowded out the former paradigm of *trivium*, which connected ethics, politics, and economics. Strongly linked to the paradigm of efficiency is the concept of *fair price as a part of contractual justice*, which now dominated disruptive justice in economics. The focus is on the formulation of mathematical methods, the functioning of the market mechanism, and the allocative efficiency of market systems. Instead, distributive justice was privatized and became part of an individual virtue (and of the market?).

In his study of the seventeenth century economics and ethics, *Sen* worked on the hidden parts of ethics within economics (Sen 1987). He distinguished between the *ethics-related view* of motivation for economic activity (represented by *Smith*, *Mill*, *Marx*, and others) and the more *technically oriented economists* like *Walras*, *Quesnay*, and *Ricardo,* among others, who focused on finding solutions to concrete economic tasks. For the *balance of economic science*, both groups of economists need to be in balance, *Sen* argued. In his 1993 lecture on ethics and the economics of finance, he classified the ethical framework of finance into *duties and consequences* (Sen 1993, pp. 204–207). He pinpoints the responsibility of a firm's management for all types of stakeholders. In his normative approach, he discussed the constraints for firms, which are needed to encourage them to deliver positive contributions to the society and nature. His ideas have given rise to the question of how private agents should assume responsibility in finance.

3.2.3 Overcoming the Separation Principle in Finance

The theorem of *universal separation* is one of the cornerstones of modern finance. It means that (risk-bearing) assets are structured as a portfolio in the same manner for all market participants. It requires perfect and complete capital markets, formulated in the *information efficiency market hypothesis* which was founded by *Fama*: "A market in which prices always 'fully reflect' available information is called 'efficient'" (Fama 1970, p. 383 and its enhancement in Fama 1991). *Fama's* focus is on the market price $P_{i,t}$ at time point t for an asset i and the subjective information vector ϕ_t*. Under these settings, the market price has a marginal distribution $f^*(P_{i,t+1} \mid \phi_t^*)$, derived from the subjective expectation of individual market participants $E^*(P_{i,t+1} \mid \phi_t^*)$. Assuming that such an expectation in the capital market exists, the market clearing (equilibrium) asset price depends on the expected rate of return of an asset ($E(r_{i,t+1})$), anticipated for a future period in order to ensure a market equilibrium. If rational expectation formation exists in the markets, *Fama's market efficiency hypothesis* (MEH) explains that the equilibrium price reflects all existing information completely and correctly. The subjective information set of each single market participant equals the objective ("true") information set of the market (*true joint distribution*):

$$f^*(P_{i,t+1} | \phi_t^*) = f(P_{i,t+1} | \phi_t), \tag{3.1}$$

from which follows:

$$\phi_t^* = \phi_t. \tag{3.2}$$

Where ϕ_t is the objective (true) information set.

What follows is the special shape of the price equation from (3.1):

$$P_{i,t} = E(P_{i,t+1}|\phi_t)/[(1 + E(r_{i,t+1}|\phi_t))]. \tag{3.3}$$

If the objective information set is complete and used in the correct manner, it follows that the expected rate of return is zero. According to *Fama*, an efficient market contains all the information of the set ϕ_t that is integrated into the market clearing prices. Given that, it follows that there is no opportunity for market participants to exploit excess returns based on the existing information set. Event studies are often applied to analyze whether the expected rate of return fits with the one reached or whether an excess return existed (McWilliams and Siegel 1997, p. 630 et seq.).

It is crucial for such an equilibrium market price solution that the distribution of future prices [$f^*(P_{i,t+1})$] is formulated by referring to the currently available information set (ϕ_t^*) which itself must represent the *objective distribution of market prices* [$f(P_{i,t+1})$] based on the currently existing information set (ϕ_t). The assumption of rational expectations has a paramount role in such a solution and requires the existence of rational decision-making by homogenous market participants. In this way, the *market price equilibrium* represents a *unique subjective information set* which itself by definition of the equilibrium concept is identical. States of disequilibria solely reflect temporary different individual information sets that will vanish when the buying and selling orders on the capital markets lead to a new market price equilibrium.

The MEH is strongly tied to the REH, which in turn is linked to the assumption of stationary distributed rates of returns (see Fig. 3.7). Due to these two pillars of modern finance, *the current market price* is the *best predictor of the future market price* as the currently available price setting information is available in the market and reflected in the market price. Information appearing only randomly and, therefore, unanticipated can lead to (unexpected) price changes, but systematic errors do not arise among market participants as the model rules them out. If the market price determines a market clearing equilibrium and a correct valuation of any market-traded asset, the distribution of future market prices is determined exogenously, i.e., it is not part of any individual transaction of a market participant alone. The *rule of big numbers* will eliminate any market price impact of individually adverse market decisions (Ross 1978, pp. 889–890).

MEH in conjunction with REH presumes that, due to the exogenously given distribution function of market prices, the task of market participants is restricted to the estimation of that particular function. It is also assumed that every market participant knows the model of asset price formation or acts as if he does. Furthermore, systematic errors in expectation formation do not exist, and active individual information gathering will be omitted due to the existence of transaction costs. The outcome of such a model is an *expectation equilibrium* that is *free of any arbitrage opportunities*. If such a model should work in practice, institutional micro market arrangements are necessary that ensure the functioning of an equilibrium based on market transactions: "How well and how quickly a market aggregates and

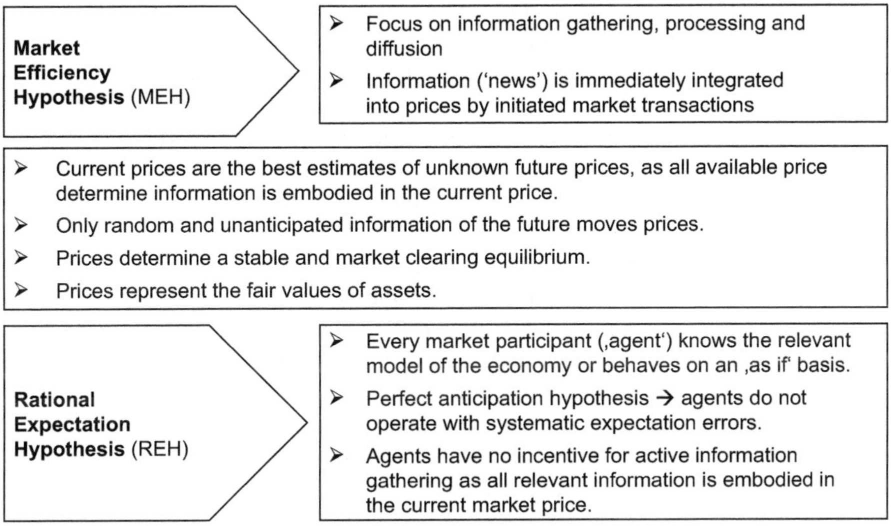

Fig. 3.7 The link between the market efficiency hypothesis (MEH) and the rational expectations hypothesis (REH)

impounds information into the price must surely be a fundamental goal of market design" (O'Hara 1995, p. 270).

The *MEH* allows the establishment of the *theorem of universal separation*. No market participant needs to focus on his individual utility function when optimizing his wealth. He can rely completely on the optimal structure of risk portfolios determined by the market equilibrium prices. This makes the consideration of *individual utility functions superfluous*. Moreover, with respect to arbitrarily stochastic distributions of returns of single assets, the optimal structure of risk portfolios is independent of the invested amount.

Another consequence is that market participants *act continuously* which makes the *time* horizon *infinite*. The resulting consequence is the *value additivity* as the most important valuation principle for assets in capital market theory and corporate finance. It states that the market value (W) of an asset (Z_3) is the result of adding up the marketed and uncorrelated weighted (q_i) values of (the present value of future cash flows) two other assets in the same market (Z_1 and Z_2). The outcome is an *arbitrage-free asset valuation* without the need to know each single market participant's utility function:

$$W(Z_3) = W(Z_1 \cdot q_1 + Z_2 \cdot q_2) = q_1 \cdot W(Z_1) + q_2 \cdot W(Z_2),\quad \text{with } q_i \neq 0 \text{ and } i = 1, 2, 3. \tag{3.4}$$

To ensure the principle in real markets, *arbitrageurs are essential*. They detect violations of the principle by comparing the *market price* of an asset with its *fair value* and equalize by buying and selling operations a temporary mismatch. Arbitrage is an investment strategy that guarantees a positive payoff (*free lunch*), in some contingency, with no possibility of a negative payoff and with no investment (i.e., it is a money pump for riskless moneymaking but with the prerequisite of acting very quickly). It makes only sense if markets are in a temporary disequilibrium. The *motivation* lies in the *self-interest* of *market participants* to take advantage of the profits coming from valuation mismatches. Important assumptions for the functioning of the arbitrage model are that there exist no informational restrictions, free information, full competition in capital markets, and the rational expectation hypothesis.

What lies behind such a *faceless market efficiency* is the assumption that market participants are represented by share- and bondholders as the two most significant groups of stakeholder when capital market transactions and the market price formation process are made. The consequences of *Fama's* idea of capital markets are tremendous. The focus on shareholders leads to the *hegemony of shareholder value maximization* and the ignorance of remaining stakeholders' interests (with the exception of debtholders). From such logic, it follows that a firm has no responsibility toward the remaining stakeholders, society as a whole (the subsystem), or toward nature (the total system).

The neoclassical inspired modelling of capital market efficiency together with rational expectations leaves no space for individuals to act differently as this would violate any economic efficient transacting. Like a law of nature, market participants follow an optimal decision path. "The behavior of economic agents is attributed to a well-defined objective—for firms it is the maximization of profits—that is pursued with complete rationality within legal and budgetary constraints. The idea (...) is used to obtain predictions of market outcomes from a minimal set of assumptions about individual participants" (Knetsch and Thaler 1986, p. 298). *Taleb* (2007, p. 228) called market participants operating in such a paradigm *slaves of fate*.

The hypothesis of *anonymous market players* operating in a *social vacuum* is disputed among economists due to the ignorance of the social aspect. Ostroy (1973, p. 597) argued: "Individuals will not exchange with the market, they will exchange with each other." *Rychen* and *Salganik* (2003) demonstrated that markets and transactions create special competences for individual participants which are the result of their *social interaction*. Under those circumstances, moral or ethical orientations cannot be neglected as they are an integral part of social networking and collaboration. However, the neoclassical-based MEH and REH approaches ignore such groundings of individual behavior in markets by setting axiomatic assumptions, and the implied overarching paradigm of *utilitarianism* serves as a hidden and forgettable ethical background. When ethics come into play, such a mechanistic world of capital markets thus described suddenly contains more elements that are human. This can be demonstrated by two examples (Soppe 2000, pp. 38–40).

3.2.3.1 Ethics and Arbitrage

The assumptions and the construction of *efficient capital markets* are implicitly embedded in a *teleological approach to ethics*: the unregulated free market process is the ultimate aim in its own right, while humans are subordinated to this higher goal and fulfill the requirements of a workable competitive market. Comparable to the *Taylor* type of manufacturing in the real economy, individuals in the MEH are condemned to acting as a well-defined machine. Confronted with the schools of ethics, the following objections against MEH and especially arbitrage can be evolved. In summary, the criticisms of *virtue ethics* are as follows:

- *Individual level*: Arbitrage is like making money for the sake of money. Individual income and wealth maximization are the sole driving force for market transactions. Both are highly reminiscent of *Aristotle*'s chrematistics. Instead of the MEH, rational market participants should be completely free to make their own informed choices, which might be relevant from their own individual perspective and to their own decision-making.
- *Collective level*: The crucial message of the MEH is the logic that an individual market participant is not able to beat capital markets (permanently). Trading on such markets follows a *zero sum game*, i.e., one person's gain is another person's loss. On the other hand, making money by arbitrage could render some kind of service to the public by making markets more efficient.

Deontological ethics could contribute to the discussion in the following way:

- Market participants should feel *morally responsible* for each other. If arbitrage is a zero sum game, then agents should only trade if both parties (buyer and seller) involved in the arbitrage gain from the transactions.
- Only then does no individual loss of welfare follow. At the collective level, ethics can create value because they sustain the necessary efficient pricing process in markets (pareto-optimum). Instead of that mechanistic view, the MEH should take the social will power of market participants into account, which is much less foreseeable with respect to the outcome predicted by the model's behavioral assumptions.

If REH and MEH are compared to critics from *virtue ethics* and *deontological ethics*, one can state:

- This joint hypothesis leaves *no room for differing individual judgments* of an investment opportunity and makes individual decision-making senseless as everything has already been determined by the market forces from which nobody can escape.
- Therefore, *all* market participants make the *same rational choices* due to the analysis of the consequences of an equal decision problem.
- The *herd*-like *effect* then is that market participants are supposed to choose the investment alternative with the highest expected return per unit of risk.

In conclusion, one can summarize that neither MEH nor REH allows any market participant to drift away from the model's decision-making process given that there is no room for individually different ethical views. Everyone is under pressure to behave in the same manner, dictated by anonymous market forces.

3.2.3.2 "Rocking" the *Modigliani/Miller* Theorem

The *Fisher* separation, *Tobin's* universal separation, *Modigliani/Miller's* theorem, and others all state: the (market) value of a firm is independent of its sources of financing. In the first hypothesis, the so-called *Modigliani/Miller mark I* declares that (market) values do not depend on the composition of the cost of capital (be it equity or debt). Therefore, the weighted average cost of capital (WACC) does not influence a firm's value, and the same is true for the financial leverage. In the *Modigliani/Miller mark II*, it is maintained that the cost of equity increases linearly through an increase in the financial leverage. Each investor is able to determine his own individual financial leverage by purchasing debt-financed shares. If investment opportunities to earn a *free lunch* exist (i.e., arbitrage is possible), a market participant will adjust his current individual financial leverage in such a way that he can purchase shares in the undervalued firm and exploit potential gains. If a firm's income taxes are included, a *tax shield effect* can be exploited, and there will be a further inducement to increase the number of debt-financed share purchases.

However, with these internationally renowned theorems, practitioners felt inspired to undertake profit making financial transactions as buyouts and other operations of private equity investors as, for instance, hedge funds have demonstrated in the past. Nevertheless, such operations can sometimes conflict with ethical positions as the following citation of *Horrigan* (1987, p. 105) states: "The advice that stockholders can just 'walk away' from financial distress actively encourages firms to court bankruptcy risks. (...), the interests of the workforce and the community in the livelihood of the firm are cynically assumed to be of little importance. The firm just represents a 'crap shoot' on a 'lottery ticket' subsidized by creditors and employees."

Chapter 4
Key Points of Sustainability and CSR: Stakeholder Theory and the Theory of External Effects

Abstract Based on the previous discussions of finance and capital market theory and their links to ethics and morality, a sketch of the pivotal role of the theory of external effects on many areas of corporate social responsibility and sustainability is presented. It is argued that the internalization of external effects in a globally integrated world faces severe shortcomings due to a governance vacuum in the enforcement of national laws and taxes. The upcoming paradigm of sustainable development together with corporate social responsibility in conjunction with stakeholder theory allows a civil society-based approach to cope with the challenges of external outcomes. Stakeholders and nongovernmental organizations are discussed as agents that could stimulate and even sanction firms to act sustainably. The threat to withdraw their licenses to operate or to co-operate plays a major role in this approach.

Keywords Corporate social responsibility · Sustainable development · External effects · *Coase* theorem · *Pigou* tax · Governance vacuum · Eco-efficiency · License to operate

With the rise of globalization, the exploitation of natural resources, the increasing interdependency between economies and societies around the globe, and the soaring social and environmental problems, the *concept of sustainability* has grabbed the world's attention over the past decades. The latest awareness is the conception of 17 Sustainable Development Goals, i.e., globally *SDGs*, published by the United Nations at the end of 2015.[1] These goals spotlight the responsibility of humankind for the survival of the own species and how to cope with the negative consequences of environmental and social threats that arise from unsustainable behavior. As *Kitzmueller* and *Shimshack* (2012) argue, the concept of sustainability has emerged to a high profile issue, and CSR has become a part of business strategies and activities in many sectors, firms, and countries. *Salzmann* (2013, pp. 557–559)

[1]https://sustainabledevelopment.un.org/sdgs

H. Schäfer, *On Values in Finance and Ethics*, SpringerBriefs in Finance,
https://doi.org/10.1007/978-3-030-04684-2_4

presents the results of research in economic scientific journals from the millennium until 2011. She concluded that sustainability in business economics has been among the most fruitful research areas and is now well established. The contributions in the scientific journals span a variety of areas and topics. The following sections give an overview of the different approaches.

4.1 Starting from the "Interior of the Earth": Neoclassical Paradigm and the Problem of External Effects

One of the basic problems of the inefficient and suboptimal allocation of resources and goods in microeconomics and business administration is *external effects*. In general, they emerge from the economic transactions or activities of an individual market participant that directly influence the well-being of another person, entity, society, or nature. External effects can lead to a *negative or positive* spillover. In addition, externalities may arise if activities of one individual affect another one. If such a spillover is not considered in the decision-making of the former, the economic activity is biased, and production and consumption processes are not (pareto-) efficient. The production of goods is either too high or too low compared to the levels of an efficient allocation in a market economy without external effects. The *concept of negative external effects* as applied in sustainability models nowadays is deeply rooted in environmental economics.

In Fig. 4.1 an example of external effects along the value chain of an electronic manufacturer is illustrated. It demonstrates the variety of external effects, which can be broken down into those with positive and negative spillovers to third parties, i.e., those who do not operate with a firm on explicit contractual relationships and the

+	The firm buys components made from recycled metals. The firm works with its suppliers to ensure that their employees are paid a living wage and are not pressured to work unreasonable hours.	The firm powers its own factories on renewable energy and exports clean energy to the grid. The firm invests in training and education of its own employees.	The firm's products provide benefits to society by being used to reduce energy consumption, deliver learning and education and/or provide medical services.
-	Suppliers discharge hazardous chemicals into the air and water, affecting the health of local communities Suppliers use child labour.	Workers are injured in accidents on the assembly line. The firm's factory emits greenhouse gases.	Products are disposed of in landfill rather than being recycled.
	Supply Chain (Upstream)	**Firm operations (Manufacturing)**	**Use and disposal of products (Downstream)**

Fig. 4.1 Positive (+) and negative (−) externalities throughout a value chain—an illustrative example (KPMG 2014, p. 13)

environment as such. Strictly speaking, the concept of external effects in stakeholder theory is *one-sided as it exclusively focuses on the negative side of external effects*—and implicitly free rides positive external effects of a firm's value chain.

To demonstrate the basic concept of external negative effects and its consideration in the theory of CSR and sustainability, the following simplified *example* is illustrative. For instance, let us consider the leather goods market. *Leather manufacturing* wastes water, and if disposed of into a river, the water would hardly be drinkable as it starts stinking and becomes muddied and toxic.

Imagine there is a *beer-garden downstream* where people like to have fun in the summer. With the stinking muddy river flowing past, few people will choose to sit in the garden and enjoy drinking beer. As they would no longer visit such a beer garden, the property owner's turnover would drop, leading to a decrease in his personal income. A strong connection between the leather good manufacturer polluting the river and his economic profits is obvious. The leather good manufacturer operates with lower costs if disposal facilities to avoid the pollution were not installed. Instead, the operating of such a facility would incur higher production costs but serves as the internalization of a negative external effect. With higher costs, the manufacturer's profit margin would decrease, leading to a lower output of leather goods or to lower sales owing to the cost-adjusted increased market price (if we assume a perfect competitive market for leather goods).

On the other hand, consumers would demand a too high quantity of leather goods if the external effects were not be internalized and therefore prices would be too low. Following Fig. 4.2 this applies at point x^0 (quantity of leather goods) with the relation of MD > (p^0 = MC). Here the marginal damage exceeds the price of the good (as determined by the marginal costs). In such cases, the price of the leather good does not correctly inform the market about the true marginal cost of the leather good production.

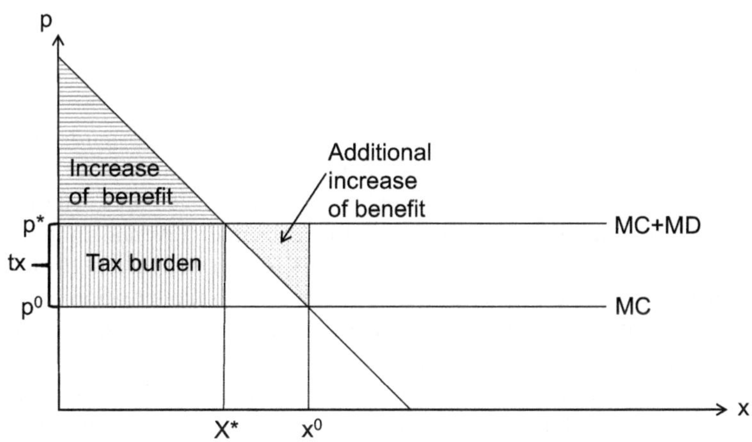

Fig. 4.2 Illustration of the economics of a negative external effect

Two questions then arise and are an integral part of *welfare economics*: How can the negative spillover be reduced or avoided, and what would be the resultant redistribution effects on the income streams of the property owner and the firm? In principle, there are *two alternative ways to solve the problem*:

- *Taxes and subsidies*. They represent a public policy instrument, centralized in the hands of the government and is known in welfare economics as the *Pigou tax*.
- By establishing of *property rights*, a market-based decentralized instrument, can be made available to private market participants, i.e., a way to internalize external effects without any interference from the government. The assumption is that the government has installed and is running a legal system which ensures the implementation of such needed property rights.

4.1.1 A Tax for Good

If the government charges a *Pigou* tax (tx), the consumer is obliged to pay the government. For the manufacturer, the cost per unit then increases to MC + tx, ideally reflecting the true cost function, just as the tax burden should exactly match the otherwise increased consumer profit (due to the lower price). The optimal tax rate is found when it equals the marginal damage (MD) and the negative external effect can be internalized. Then the manufacturer sets a price equal to the *public marginal costs*, i.e., $p^* = \text{MC} + \text{tx} = \text{MC} + \text{MD}$, corresponding with the reduced quantity of goods (x^*). The result would be a *pareto-efficient production and consumption*. An actual pareto-efficient improvement (compared to the inefficient result without a tax) demands a reimbursement of the tax income and can be accelerated by additional compensations (Pigou 2002, p. 184).

4.1.2 A Market for "Bads"

Let us now assume that the leather good manufacturer and the beer-garden owner fill their pockets with the entire consumer revenues (this assumption is for the sake of simplification). In Fig. 4.2 this is indicated by the dark-shaded area. The manufacturer achieves a profit by the amount of the consumer revenue in the market equilibrium. The owner of the beer-garden suffers from a decrease in his profits by the amount of the negative external effect (compared to the situation without the manufacturer's pollution). The crucial question now is about the definition of *property rights*, which allow the property owner to sell the manufacturer an entitlement giving him the right to pour wastewater into the river. The *crucial question* would then be how much the manufacturer would be willing to pay in order to gain the wastewater entitlement for one unit of leather good manufactured. A related question is: What is the minimum the beer-garden property owner wants to earn through the sale of such an entitlement, and how much waste in the river is he willing to accept?

The ***Coase*** *theorem* states that inefficiencies like external effects can arise in a market system if the affected parties do not start negotiations, even though a pareto-efficient improvement would, in fact, be possible for them.[2] The definition of property rights can facilitate such negotiations and lead to an efficient solution, which would be the ideal case from a neoclassical point of view. It would optimize the market allocation of goods. Critics often point out that transaction costs might destroy any possible bargaining solution between two parties. Such costs could arise for the opening and maintaining of such a market, the costs of negotiations between the parties, and the costs of the law enforcement (particularly concerning the jurisdiction). As *Coase* (1960, p. 43) pointed out: "In order to carry out a market transaction it is necessary to discover who it is that one wishes to deal with, to inform people that one wishes to deal and on what terms, to conduct negotiations (...) undertake inspection (...) These operations are often extremely costly, sufficiently costly (...) to prevent many transactions that would be carried out in a world in which the pricing system worked without costs."

Indeed, in practice, it does matter whether and how property rights are defined, since different national legal systems with different associated transaction costs are decisive for an economic relevant solution. Here the *transaction cost theory* has to specify how such costs can be reduced to allow market solutions for, generally speaking, many different purposes. If *property rights* cannot be installed, we have to admit a market failure. Other reasons would be that the exclusion principle cannot be applied, or there is no rivalry in consumption. If both of these conditions exist for a good, it takes on the character of a public good. The government should supply it instead of the market. The *Pigou* tax might be understood as an instrument that should be applied if markets cannot be opened and operated. What happens if not only markets fail but governments as well? Since the beginning of globalization with free market entries for firms in many national markets around the world, the mobility of capital has become a fact, and firms have many incentives to switch between countries to exploit the best economic and tax conditions for the settlement of production plants and sales forces. National laws end at the border and that is true for *Pigou* taxes, too.

In the era of globalization, changing global supplier structures, intense competition, and cost pressures together with the transformation of production and value-added processes often dramatically affect stakeholder expectations and demands. With borderless firms, national laws are no longer able to protect stakeholder rights efficiently. Therefore, owing to a lack of regulations, firms can take profitable advantage of such opportunities for the sake of stakeholders (regulation arbitrage). Although the national regulator is aware of such exploitations, it is often not possible to internalize the negative effects just by national law. Then a kind of "*governance vacuum*" emerges (Beck 1992; Giddens 1998). At that point, there needs to be a

[2]The following part is based on the interpretation of *Cheung* (1973).

differentiation between legality and legitimacy with regard to a firm's behavior and responsibility. *Legitimacy* in the sense of ethical acceptance is the prerequisite for building and maintaining a positive firm reputation (Louche 2004, p. 70). According to the knowledge-based theory of the firm, reputation is an *intangible resource* and can serve as a strategic dynamic capability. To gain and to maintain reputation thus could have an economic value (see also Sect. 5.1).

Many firms have learned to cope with regulations and tax burdens by circumventing country-specific tax regulations and exploiting national public subsidies (*tax arbitrage*), so that a governance vacuum on the regulator's side is quite apparent. In democratic systems, the state's governance vacuum with respect to a firm's behavior on a global scale could become a severe challenge for stakeholders. In such cases, past developments have demonstrated that *civil society institutions* with NGOs as their spearhead can partly make up for the government's (weakened) role (Besley and Ghatak 2007):

- Under the premises of globalization, governance vacuum, and highly mobile capital, *CSR*, can, on the one hand, be understood as a concept that *delivers instruments for stakeholders*. If national government laws are limited to their country's borders, NGOs can put pressures on firms toward internalizing negative external effects. But the enforcement of environmental and social firm policies by NGOs can never be a substitute for laws. In a democratic system NGOs have no mandates grounded on the will of citizens that is justified by democratic elections. Insofar *NGOs* are operating *between governments and markets* (and would require an extraordinary monitoring by governments and civil society).
- On the other hand, *CSR* could be understood as the *source of firms' 'voluntarily' activities by partially offering private goods* (in the sense of club goods) to selected stakeholders with whom the firm would like to collaborate. Economic incentives for such a collaboration on the firm side can be the improvement of products, an eased marketing of innovations, and the strengthening of the firm's competitiveness in contestable markets (Kitzmueller and Shimshack 2012, pp. 57–60).

4.2 The Concept of Sustainable Development and Its Links to Finance

With the transformation of most of the former socialist-communist countries to market economies in the 1990s, the significance and role of *ethics and morality in economic life* experienced a *renaissance*. By comparison, the recapitulation of morality and ethics in capital markets and finance started rather late. The *bridging* of the *gap between finance and ethics* has been accomplished in the last four decades mainly through asset allocation strategies and policies. Having started from investment styles that follow a deontological approach and excluded "*sin stocks*," i.e., refused to invest in controversial sectors and firms like arms producers, adult entertainment, and alcohol manufacturers, more sophisticated approaches emerged called "positive investments," "thematic investments," "impact investments," "engagement," and "best in class" (Schäfer 2012). From a technical point of view, *new rating schemes* were developed that assess a firm's (and government's) contribution and violation regarding ethical environmental, social, and governance issues and aggregated the results to an overall *sustainability rating score* (Schäfer 2009).

A *cornerstone* of such *sustainability ratings* until present is *environmental issues*. It is a result of early discussions about the capital markets' roles in a natural environment whose capacity of dealing with pollution seems increasingly exhaustible. Besides the problem of exhausted resources that occurred, it had been detected by several empirical analyses starting in the 1970s, such as the *Limits to Growth* of the Club of Rome (Meadows et al. 1972) and academic research on exhaustible natural resource and economic growth (e.g., Baumol 1968; Stiglitz 1974).

On the eve of globalization, the development of new products, the dynamic economic development of emerging markets, and erratic technological innovations, *Barbara Ward*, founder of the "International Institute for Environment and Development," was the first to formulate the term *sustainable development*. She claimed that the social and economic development had to go hand in hand with the protection and conservation of nature (Dalal-Clayton 1999, p. 1).

In 1987 the United Nations installed the World Commission of Environment and Development (WCED), chaired by the former Norwegian Prime Minister *Gro Harlem Brundtland*. The so-called *Brundtland Commission* formulated the concept of sustainable development with a clear-cut *anthropogenic impetus*, which displaced the former eco-centric concept (World Commission of Environment and Development 1987, p. 24). Together with the following United Nations Conference on Environment and Development (UNCED) in Rio de Janeiro in 1992, sustainability was reformulated as a *concept of justice*—between existing generations (*intragenerational justice*, e.g., the distribution of wealth and income between developed and emerging nations) and between present and future generations (*intergenerational justice*) (Atkinson 2000).[3] Since then, the term *sustainable development* has been adopted as an internationally acknowledged normative guiding principle in politics and economics, manifested in the Rio declaration. Sustainability at its core needs to be understood as an ethically related concept and has a double ethical imperative with a strong link to *Aristotle's oikonomia*—the resilience of natural capital and the sufficiency of social capital (Daly 1991, p. 29).

Although the findings of the *Brundtland* Commission remained vague in many parts and led to a *profusion* of definitions and interpretations of the term *sustainability*, the conceptualization of sustainability spread over to politicians, managements, and societies (Pearce and Atkinson 1998). Today there seems to be a lasting *consensus* that the concept of sustainability has to be materialized in *environmental*,

[3] "Sustainable development is the development that meets the needs of the present without compromising the ability of future generations to meet their own needs" (WCED 1987, p. 54).

economic, and *social dimensions* (see Fig. 4.3). However, critical questions associated with the concept have been left unanswered until today. Therefore, the most important question for the intragenerational justice of the concept is what distribution is sufficiently fair when referring to such aspects as equality, needs, and performance. Intergenerational justice seems to be challenged most by the question of what should be passed on according to individual and collective assessments.

What often seems to be overlooked or misconstrued in the sustainability concept is that it does not represent a well-defined term in the sense of a constitutive idea. Application by politicians, managers, and others is therefore not straightforward. It has many more parallels to a regulative idea in the *Kantian* sense or is like a mission statement referring to *inter- and intragenerational justice*. It should stimulate searching and learning processes within society and science, without any advance descriptions of objects and methods. The *concept of sustainability* has a greater relationship to *heuristics and continuous advancement*, even when elaborating on the definition of the term itself.

The most important development in the field of sustainability was the signing of the *Kyoto Protocol*, a framework convention on climate change by several industrialized nations, at the United Nations in 1997 (United Nations Framework Convention on Climate Change 1998). With it, the public and academic discussion of the concept of sustainable development was narrowed down to the question of how to cope with the *worldwide effects of greenhouse gases* and *man-made climate change*. The increase in *global warming*, causing extreme weather events,

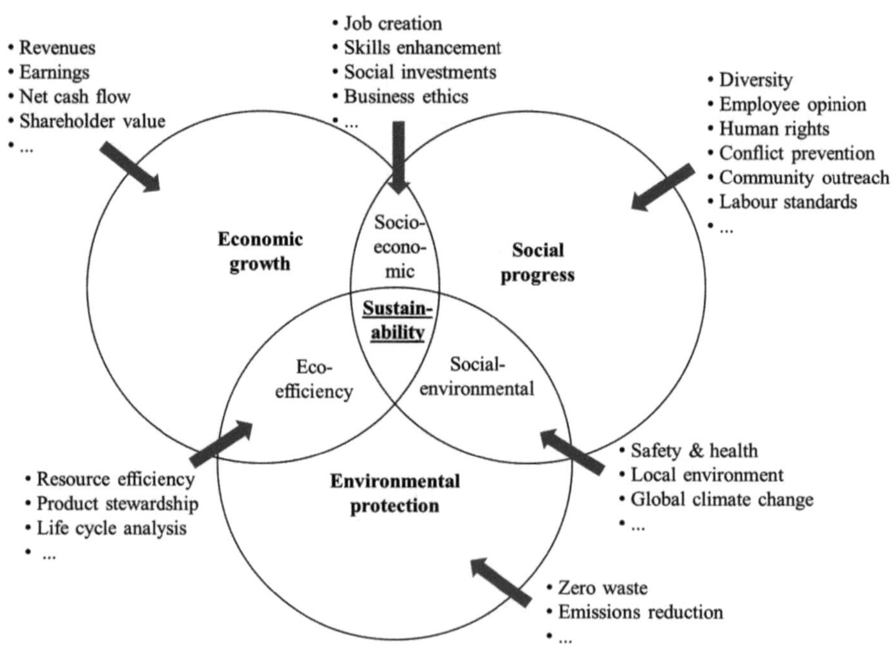

Fig. 4.3 Sustainable development: application of an evolutionary concept

desertification, water shortages, etc., has become a top issue in many political and economic agendas. Studies of the Intergovernmental Panel on Climate Change warn of the disastrous consequences of the greenhouse gas effect (IPCC 2007). The *Stern Report* (Stern 2007) made it clear that the economic challenge will be immense and that capital markets have to carry the biggest burden to finance the conversion of economies to greater climate-friendliness. There exist many studies that try to estimate the investment volume of adaption and mitigation strategies to cope with climate change, e.g., the estimates ordered by the G20 Group: during a period of 15 years, USD 90 trn must be spent worldwide to ensure an environment-friendly development (New Climate Economy 2016). Financing sustainability not only appears as a necessity in order to impede climate change but also as an opportunity for firms to participate in a *Kontratieff cycle of new technologies* and *innovative products* to cover long-lasting needs (Schmidheiny and Zorraquin 1996). Financial markets should become aware of the threats and opportunities of climate change as one part of the sustainable development with the highest priority. Such an enhanced understanding of the financial sector's role is accompanied by demands of international institutions to contribute to the transition of current economic systems to *green economies*: "It is clear that across banking, investment and insurance—the core activities of the financial system—significant changes in philosophy, culture, strategy and approach, notably the overwhelming dominance of short-termism, will be required if capital and finance is to be reallocated to accelerate the emergence of a green economy" (UNEP 2011, p. 44).[4]

The former United Nations (UN) secretary *Kofi Annan* achieved the trailblazing link to the concept of sustainable development in financial markets. In the spring of 2006, he announced the *United Nations Principles for Responsible Investments* (PRI) following the already developed concept of the *UN Environmental Program for the Finance Initiative* (UNEP FI). Currently, more than 1700 signatories like asset managers, financial intermediaries, etc. have signed the six Principles for Responsible Investments, representing assets worth USD 70 trn under their management worldwide. Signees of the PRI draw upon the capacity of investors and capital markets in general to make prominent contributions to the sustainable development of the globe by setting progressive environmental, social, and governance goals for the asset management of firms and public authorities.

Today we can say that the concept of sustainable development is an interdependent model for maintaining resources and substances. From a political point of view, it is about the internalization of negative externalities through public regulations (mostly taxes) and market-driven (*Coase*) solutions. One of the most prominent realizations of the market-based concept is the organized trading of emission allowances, e.g., represented by the *Emission Trading Scheme* of the *European Union (EU-ETS)*. In addition, they are demonstrations of the related

[4]"A green economy (GE) can be defined as one that results in improved human well-being and social equity, while significantly reducing environmental risks and ecological scarcities" (UNEP 2011, p. 4).

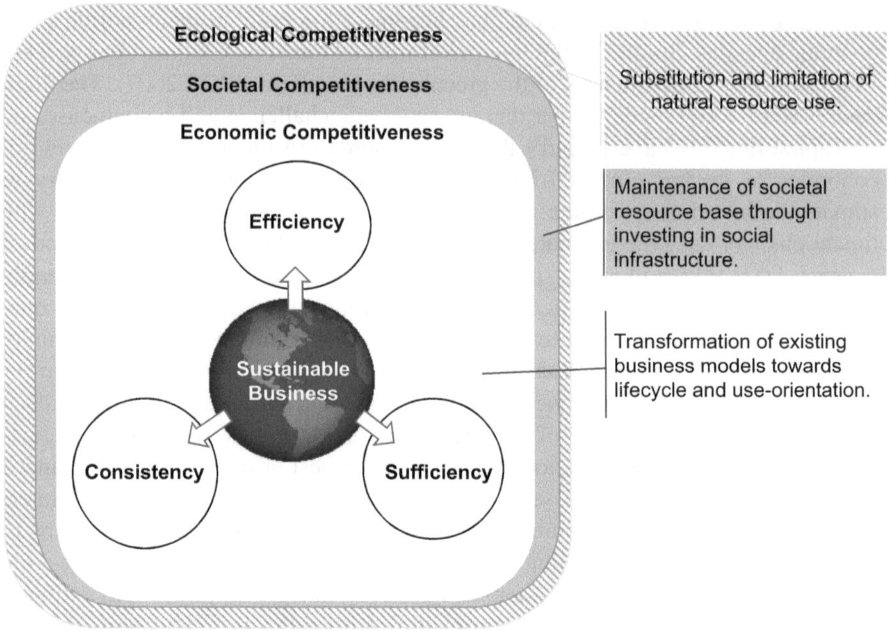

Fig. 4.4 Sustainability resulting from efficiency, sufficiency, and consistency and their roles for the competiveness of an economic system

challenges of such a new and workable market establishment. From the beginning, the EU-ETS has been accompanied by several severe problems, mostly about the *cap-and-trade mechanism*, *fraud of market participants in the case of value-added tax*, and the *bargaining of industrial sectors* with the European Commission concerning the endowment of free emission allowances, etc. (Creti et al. 2012, p. 327).

Society opinion highlights that a *sustainable development* is a prerequisite for the survival of future generations (intergenerational justice) and for the well-being of existing generations (intragenerational justice). There seems to be *little doubt among* an increasing number of *firms* that such aspects are also *highly relevant* to business models and actually for the survivorship of firms as institutions. From a firm-related organizational way of thinking, the concept of sustainability should be understood as a bundle of opportunities to combine improvements of the nature and society with advantages of strengthened competitiveness, progress in the management of risks, and last but not least a strengthened financial performance.

The concept of sustainable development rests upon three pillars—*sufficiency*, *efficiency*, and *consistency*. From an economic point of view, these three pillars can be understood as contributors to the competitiveness of an economic macro and micro system as demonstrated in Fig. 4.4.

Often associated with *sufficiency* are popular opinions like "getting enough—thinking about what you really need and stopping before you are full." The current state of individuals' welfare is the benchmark for extending or intensifying economic activities. The focus here is on the conservation of the use of resources. Nowadays sufficiency is intensively discussed on the macro level as a benchmark for the so-called *qualitative growth of* an entire *economy* that reduces exhausting scarce resources and is seen as the main prerequisite for a qualitative welfare (Nordhaus and Tobin 1972). Related to efficiency is the preservation of resources, which can also be translated as maintaining economic *substance*.

For years, the term "substance" on the microlevel has been an integral part of management theory and business administration, but with a sole link to the *single bottom line*. It has a strictly financial purpose: maintaining the favorable natural capital substance of a firm as a precondition to generating profits and to reinvestment (which itself is the precondition for value creating sources to allow the generation of profits)—i.e., nothing more than a firm's survival. This marks a fundamental link to the concept of sustainable development.

An *efficiency strategy of economic activities* intends to achieve a higher level of economic and societal welfare with a constant input of resources. The leverage is the more efficient usage of existing (exhaustible) resources. The concept of *ecological efficiency* allows the reduction of waste within an environment-friendly project in different parts of the value chain throughout the entire operating phases, (1 to *n*) as is commonly defined in the following relationship (Buritt and Schaltegger 2001):

$$\text{Ecological efficiency} = \frac{\sum_{n}^{1} \begin{array}{l}\text{Reduced ecological damage during}\\ \text{the lifelong operation measured in}\\ \text{units of damage creation(DC)}\end{array}}{\sum_{n}^{1} \begin{array}{l}\text{Damage creation caused during}\\ \text{production, operating and disposal}\\ \text{of an environmental-friendly project in}\\ \text{units of damage creation(DC)}\end{array}} \qquad (4.1)$$

Closely related to ecological efficiency is the concept of *economic-ecological ('eco') efficiency*. It requires an increase in the net reduction of environmental damage (i.e., the difference between the reduction of damage during an investment project's lifetime minus the creation of damage during the production, operation and the waste disposal related to the cost of an environment-friendly project):

$$\text{Economic-ecological efficiency} = \frac{\begin{array}{c}\text{Net reduction of ecological damages}\\ \text{measured in damage units (DU)}\end{array}}{\begin{array}{c}\text{Costs of environment-friendly}\\ \text{projects in monetary units (MU)}\end{array}} \qquad (4.2)$$

From a firm's point of view, the concept of *eco-efficiency* has attracted the greatest interest as it promises a *simultaneous improvement* in both the *financial* and *ecological outcome* of economic activities. By reducing energy and resource inputs per unit of produced goods, a firm's total costs can decline. Ideal would be a

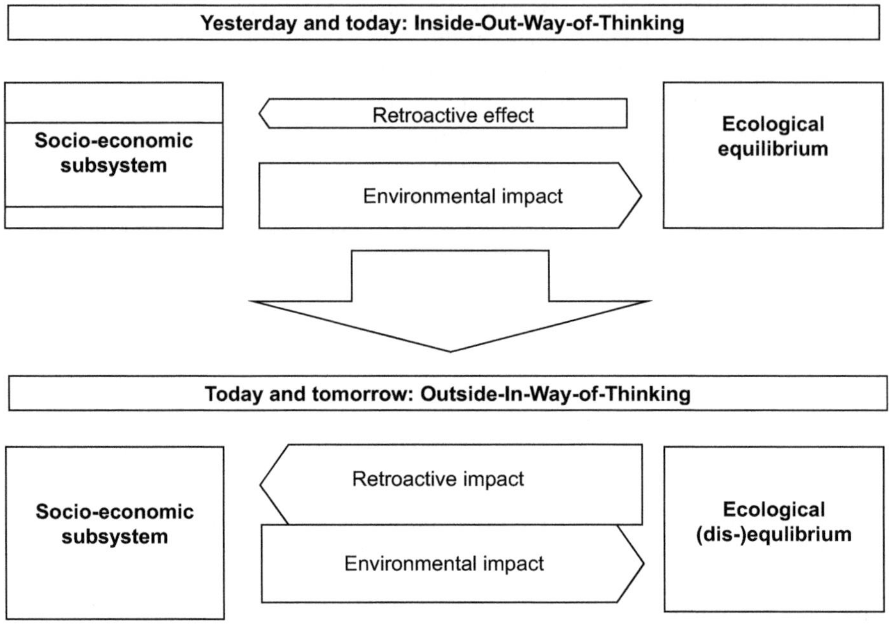

Fig. 4.5 Sustainability myopia

resulting *pareto-optimal situation*: Lower costs could drive higher profits compared to a constant turnover. Nature would gain as fewer resources and energy per product unit are needed and overall less greenhouse gas would be emitted.

However, for the well-being of nature and societies and for the preservation of tangible resources for production and consumption, eco-efficiency would only help, if the units of resources and energy saved remained in nature. If instead (as has often happened in the past) resources saved are reinvested in the economy in order to increase production or to be consumed, *eco-efficiency contributes little to sustainable development*. If society, economy, and nature are no longer able to provide the resources necessary for enduring a high-level production, a quantitative growth could only be preserved if firms invest in projects that sustain the reproduction of the vital resources necessary for the future survival of humanity.

Nowadays the relevance of the concept of *sustainable development* as an enabler for the survival of humanity and nature is often in *competition* with the *negative consequences* of modern ongoing unsustainable ways of life and the way production and consumption occur. As the earth's capacity (i.e., to provide resources and to absorb emissions) seems to be in constant decline, the accompanying negative effects are bringing the ecological system more and more into an imbalance with negative impacts on socioeconomic subsystems (see Fig. 4.5). Climate change, energy shortages, and other unsustainable events in the recent past might serve as a demonstration for such apprehension. Secretary-General *Ban Ki-moon* of the United Nations Headquarters' statement in a speech made at the KPMG summit

"Business Perspective For Sustainable Growth on 14th February 2012" is impressive:

> We are at a critical juncture—economically, socially and environmentally:
>
> - More than one billion people lack access to food, electricity or safe drinking water.
> - Most of the world's ecosystems are in decline.
> - The gap between rich and poor is widening.
> - We are nearing the point of no return on climate change.
> - The threat to prosperity, productivity and stability is clear.
> - (...)
> - A series of disasters, scandals and business-as-usual have made people increasingly skeptical of the corporate world.
> - The future of markets is under debate. But one thing is clear: we need markets that can deliver a sustainable and equitable future for all.
> - Many argue whether capitalism is in crisis. Others call this a crisis of globalization.
> - What I see is a crisis of leadership—a lack of imagination in looking at old problems with fresh eyes—and a lack of urgency as the clock keeps ticking.
> - In these uncertain and tumultuous times, we need to work together to deliver solutions for sustainability. (Ban Ki-moon 2012)

This brings us closer to the pessimistic results for future resource availability, waste reduction, etc. stemming from the follow-up report of the *Club of Rome* (Meadows et al. 1972, 2009), as *Dennis Meadows*, the leading capacity of the study, formulated in an interview for the Swiss financial newspaper *Finanz und Wirtschaft*: "Today everyone talks about Sustainable Development. This is irrelevant because the ecological capacity has been greatly exceeded. We should talk about Resilience instead—which means how shock resistant development would be possible" (Meadows 2009, p. 25).[5] The sharp increase in mega and systemic risks (OECD 2003; Renn and Klinke 2004) like climate change-induced hurricanes, tsunamis, etc. is a dramatic illustration of this point of view and raises doubts as to whether there is enough willingness, capacity, and time to avoid tipping points with irreversible negative consequences as, e.g., the *World Bank report* on *climate change* has warned (World Bank 2012). Thus for a growing number of firms, the concept of *resilience* seems more and more an inevitable complement to sustainability as a guiding principle.

4.3 Corporate Social Responsibility (CSR): A Twin to Sustainability?

"CSR is concerned with treating the stakeholders of a firm ethically or in a socially responsible manner. Stakeholders exist both within a firm and outside it. Consequently, behaving socially responsibly will increase the human development of

[5]The original interview was given in German language. The English translation was done by the book's author, Henry Schäfer.

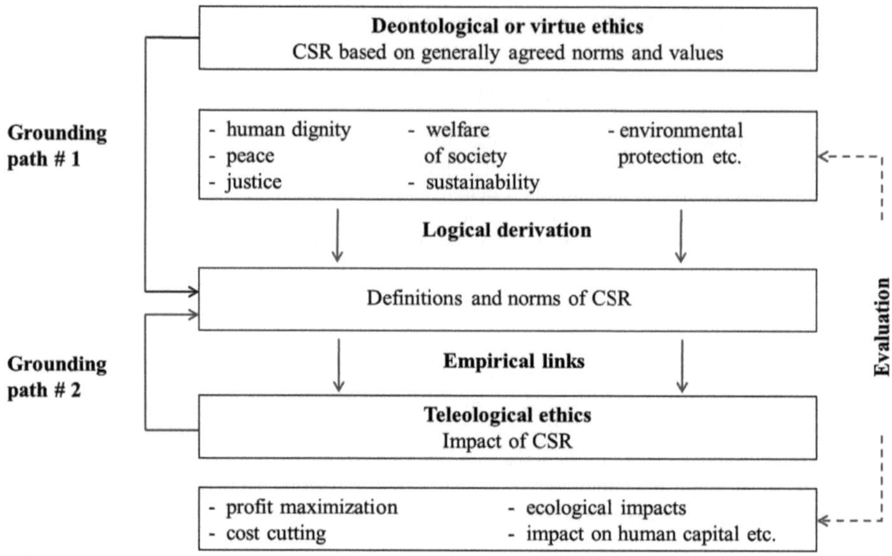

Fig. 4.6 The ethical groundings of CSR (Küpper 2006, p. 170)

stakeholders both within and outside the corporation" (Hopkins 1998, p. 14). Comparable to the broad variety of interpretations and comprehensions of the term *sustainability*, the definitions of *CSR* are also manifold, and a variety of definitions and *approaches exist in parallel* (Carroll 1999; e.g., Garriga and Melé 2004, for a comprehensive review). In general, *CSR* means actions by firms towards society and the environment over and above their legal obligations, i.e., it is about firms voluntarily meeting their social responsibility. From an academic point of view, the understanding of CSR could either be based on *deontological and virtue ethics*, should norms and guidelines be considered, telling firms what they need to do to be "good." Another fundamental can be distinguished by focusing on the possible impacts of firms' economic activities. In the *teleological sense*, CSR should then avoid any damage to the environment or in social life (see Fig. 4.6). From a traditional standpoint and as a general principle, CSR is understood in the sense of an honest and moral "businessman," engaged in "*society's general wellbeing*" (Bowen 1953, p. 6).

Today CSR is used as a *generic term*. In his survey, *Dahlsrud* (2008, p. 4) concluded that the definitions of CSR mostly refer to issues like the environment, social responsibility, stakeholders, autocracy, and efficiency. In their 2011 updated "new definition" of CSR, the EU Commission has stressed the responsibility of firms toward society: "To fully meet their CSR, firms should have in place a process to integrate social, environmental, ethical, human rights and consumer concerns into their business operations and core strategy in close collaboration with their stakeholders."[6] Meanwhile the European Commission has followed the interpretation of CSR as the specific policies of firms to manage additional nonfinancial environmental, social, and governance objectives.[7] Abbreviated as *ESG*, the aforementioned *triad*, *environmental*, *social*, and *governance*, is the most obvious common sense referring to both.[8]

With the concepts of CSR and sustainability at the firm level (*corporate sustainability, see* Atkinson 2000), a sometimes competing twin of concept and understanding emerged in the last 20 years. In principle they have different roots, but nevertheless are very similar in the way they are applied in daily business (Reed 2001). At the *firm level*, it encompasses policies to manage environmental, social, and governance objectives (ESG issues). Such an approach fits in with the so-called *narrow neoclassical economic view of CSR*: Firms commit themselves to CSR as they are motivated by extrinsic monetary incentives due to a strong business case for CSR and the resulting competitive advantages of long-term benefits (Margolis and Walsh 2003). A *broader view* of CSR argues that public and private politics can arise that put pressure on firms, which could lead to a decline in turnover, profits, and share prices and thus force firms to correct their environmental or social outcomes (Paul and Siegel 2006).

To formulate ESG objectives and strategies and to derive appropriate activities for a firm is mostly *stakeholder-related* and *dynamic*. A firm builds up *social capital* that can be an important part of a firm's strategic dynamic capabilities. In turn, it should allow the exploitation of future competitive advantages and generate higher cash flows (Fombrum et al. 2000; Russo and Fouts 1997). Stakeholder theory then addresses the question of whether there is a link between corporate social performance (CSP) comprising the measured quality of stakeholder management and corporate financial performance (CFP), gauging the financial success of the overall business. In many areas, CSR overlaps with related concepts like corporate governance and corporate citizenship. From an accounting point of view, these approaches have in common the measurement of a firm's performance beyond the single bottom line, which reflects its sole financial performance. ESG issues are incorporated in a triple bottom line reporting (Elkington 1998). The integrated reporting approach materializes such a concept into an upcoming new accounting standard (PWC 2016). However, they are not the subject of the task in hand. Figure 4.7 demonstrates the structural relationship of these concepts.

One of the most *controversial aspects of* the *CSR* concept (and the same is true for the sustainability concept) is the question of *which* ESG issues *count the most*. As

---

[6]EC (2011, p. 6).

[7]Corporate sustainability, corporate social responsibility, corporate responsibility, or (good) corporate citizenship are often used in the same meaning (Berry et al. 2003, p. 2).

[8]The term "ESG" was coined by *Ivo Knoepfel* in his report "Who Cares Wins" (2004), which was initiated by the former UN Secretary-General Kofi Annan. The report was the first in which asset managers, bankers, and insurance manager explained why environmental, social, and governance (ESG) factors in capital markets are able to combine business with a better environment and welfare in societies.

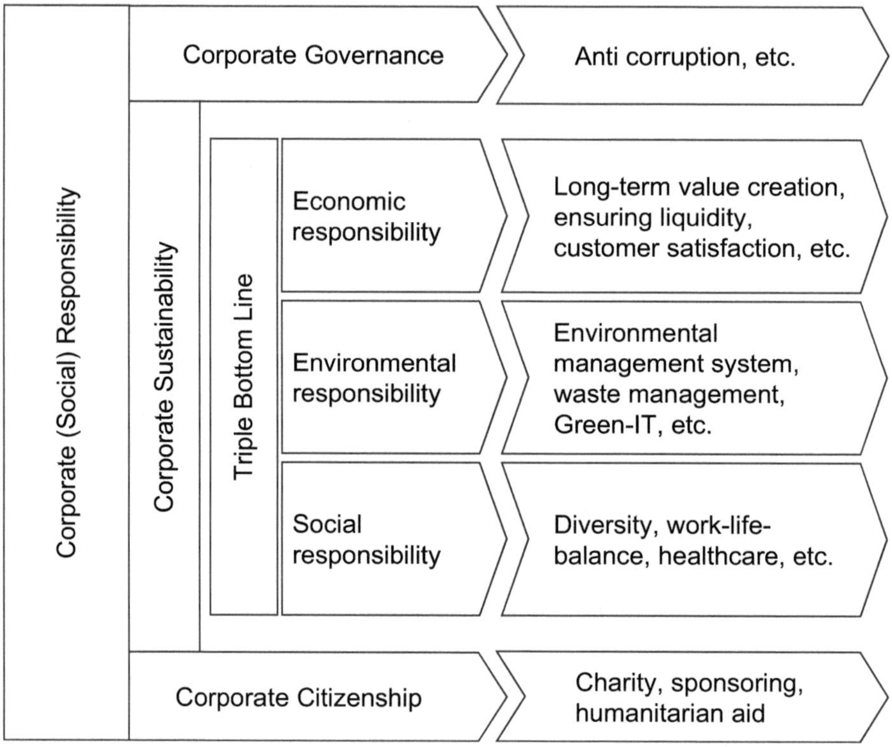

Fig. 4.7 CSR and related concepts

these concepts are ultimately based on ethical positions, answering such a question is strongly linked to institutions and/or individuals that could define the relevant ethical position. Currently many industrialized countries have *no central institution* authorized *to state what is right and what is wrong*, what the most urgent issues are, and which ones could be postponed for the future. So societies, politicians, managers, and even stakeholders are condemned to finding their own consensus about CSR's relevant issues and priorities. In addition, as this is the case, it can be argued that, nowadays, in many countries even former exponents of morality like the Church or governments are no longer monopolists in ethics and morality in the minds of average people.

Strictly speaking, ethics and morality are *private affairs*. Nevertheless, there are ways of finding out what people are worried about, what should be tackled immediately, and what could be postponed. International organizations like the United Nations, forums like the *World Economic Forum*, and other panels attempt to uphold discussions about CSR and sustainability. Figure 4.8 exhibits as an example the most important CSR and sustainability issues that were responded in two surveys, which were undertaken in different years (2009 and 2012). As has been demonstrated, priorities change over time, and new issues appear, while others have disappeared or

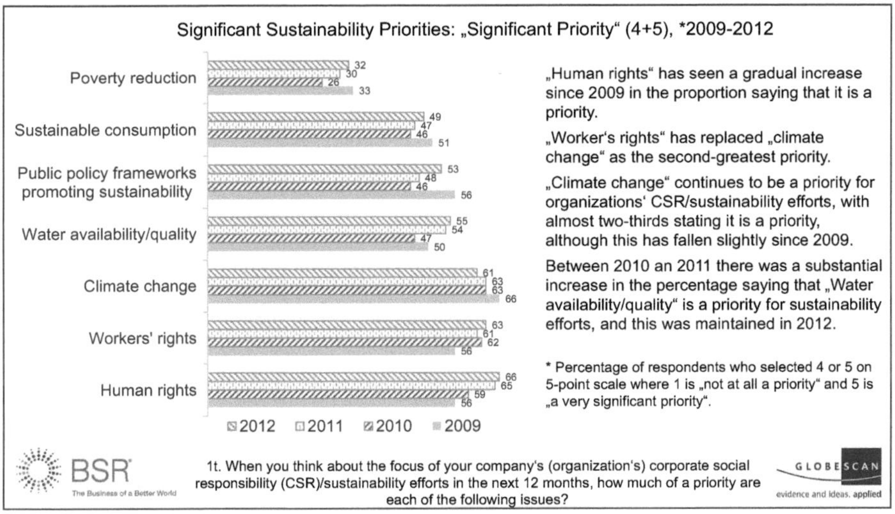

Fig. 4.8 CSR issues according to surveys—an example (Globescan and BSR 2012, p. 13)

became of lower relevance. The respondents have come from very different institutions like firms, universities, ministries, or NGOs from all over the world and should provide an approximate representation of the world's intellectual population.

During the last years on the firm level and inspired by the *materiality approach* in sustainability of one of the leading ESG reporting standards—the *Global Reporting Standard* (GRI)—*stakeholder dialogues* serve as the main sources for firms to investigate into the ESG issues that should be most relevant for them (Global Reporting Initiative 2015).

Chapter 5
Understanding How Stakeholders Are Affecting Sustainability and Finance

Abstract Contrary to the long-standing pretext that social costs would be a burden to the monetary value of firms and assets, the modern knowledge-based theory of the firm offers promising new perceptions of the links between ethics and finance. As most of the financially successful firms have proven in the recent past, strategic resources, networking, and openness to nonfinancial value drivers have the potential to create shareholder value in accordance with an appreciation of a stakeholder's well-being. The basic elements of the modern theory of the firm are reviewed in order to demonstrate that forming a link between stakeholder interests and a firm's economic goals is feasible. In an uncertain and turbulent environment, ecological, social, and governance issues together with stakeholder collaboration can gain the attributes of intangible resources that allow the value of investments and firms to thrive. Under those circumstances, a path to a conciliation between ethics, economics, and finance seems promising.

Keywords Stakeholder · Nongovernmental organization · Knowledge-based theory of the firm · Dynamic capabilities · Real options · Intangibles · Reputation

Latest with the breakdown of the Iron Curtain and the confession of failure of most of the former communistic countries in the 1990s, the capitalistic system dominates most national economic systems (Hofstede 1997). The "winds of change" established big, powerful firms representing the incarnation of globalism. Firms like Amazon, Microsoft, Google, Apple, and Facebook have grown to *global leviathans* operating borderless and switching between different national legal systems. Besides this development, a new thinking in the civil society manner evolved which can be described as *stakeholderism*. It is often understood as a countervailing power to the sharp increase of the power of firms.

It was *Freeman* (1984) who made the point about stakeholders – e.g., employees, suppliers, customers, communities, environmentalists, and human rights advocates – as being new target groups alongside share-, bond-, and debtholders. *Tirole* (2001, p. 3) called such an economic agent a *stakeholder by design*. From a macro point of view, it is often argued that such an orientation would be essential to prosperity and

H. Schäfer, *On Values in Finance and Ethics*, SpringerBriefs in Finance,
https://doi.org/10.1007/978-3-030-04684-2_5

competitiveness in the twenty-first century. Notwithstanding, *agency theory* still ignores a broader understanding of stakeholders and assigns share- and bondholders solely to the role of a principal. However, during the 1990s, convictions arose that *stakeholders* might *affect* business objectives *and* can be *critical* to a firm's financial success and contest the shareholders' demands for a firm's free cash flows (Carroll and Buchholtz 2008; Donaldson and Preston 1995). Investors would then operate in the *Freeman* sense as critical stakeholders for a firm's management. The discussion about the role and the impact of stakeholders paved the path to sustainability that is currently dominating academic discussions and efforts in practice, the *responsibility of a firm*, i.e., its management, to provide and sustain a socially and ecologically habitable environment.

Capital market theory commonly envisages shareholders as the dominating stakeholders due to their property rights and their liability in the case of a firm's default. Next to debtholders, they both provide the necessary *liquidity and capital* for the functioning of *value creating processes* in firms. Both groups of stakeholders base their investment decisions on the strict quantitative trade-off between expected return and risk, outlined in models of standard capital market theory. As these models are commonly judged as (ethical) value-free, shareholders and debtholders are assumed to solely maximize their utility in the *Fisherian* sense, i.e., they maximize their income streams out of the firm to satisfy their impatience to consume.

Moreover, such a notion of the *firm* as an *ethical value-free cash flow generation system* fits well with the *disregarding* of the *external negative effects* caused by the value creating processes of a firm – upstream and downstream. Managers are expected to act as agents of share- and debtholders in order to satisfy their income demands but ignoring the interests of third parties. In this sense, managers do not have to worry about the social or environmental costs of their daily work. Such a conception of management in terms of agency theory implicitly adheres to *teleological ethics* (especially utilitarianism). It is often accentuated by a famous citation of the Nobel laureate *Milton Friedman*: "Few trends could so thoroughly undermine the very foundations of our free society as the acceptance by corporate officials of a social responsibility other than to make as much money for their stockholders as possible." It is intriguing to contrast this citation with one of another respectable Nobel laureate, *Paul Samuelson*: "A large corporation these days not only may engage in social responsibility, it had damn well better try to do so" (Samuelson 1971, p. 24). Both refer to manager-led firms listed on stock exchanges but draw their different conclusions from their individual and controversial understanding of a firm's role with respect to stakeholder. Figure 5.1 is demonstrating the variety of areas and outcomes from the point of view of a firm that is engaged in stakeholder-oriented activities.

	Areas of stakeholder management		
	Market environment (external market stakeholders)	**Workplace (intra-firm stakeholders)**	**Social environment (external non-market stakeholders)**
Objectives (selected)	• consumer protection • fairness among market participants (e.g. commodity prices in developing countries)	• work-life-balance • equality of opportunity • participation of employees	• environmental protection • nearby infrastructure (e.g. continuing education, research)
Instruments (selected)	• seals of quality • quality management systems • cause-related marketing	• transition to flexible working hours • gender activities • involvement of employees	• energetic construction of buildings • corporate volunteering • sponsoring/social donation
Internal benefits (selected)	• differentiation from market competitors • fair sales approach	• motivation/ commitment of employees • development of employees	• cost-effectiveness (e.g. reduction of energy costs) • image benefit
Stakeholders (selected)	• customers • suppliers	• employees • investors	• ecological groups • public
Stakeholder demands (selected)	• facilitated access to product information • product safety	• rewards for exceptional • creativity/assignment of • employees	• reduction of a firm`s environmental impacts

Fig. 5.1 Objectives, instruments, and benefits of a sustainability-related stakeholder management (Maaß et al. 2014, p. 22)

5.1 Why Should Firms Care About CSR, Stakeholders, and NGOs? A Knowledge-Based View

"A firm should care about its social and environmental impacts" is a statement that very often can be heard in the media, among NGOs and from politicians. Instead, many people still believe that firms are reluctant to follow such demands as they would face additional costs and finally an adverse effect on profits, shareholder values, and share prices. Sell-side and buy-side analysts followed such a causality and often downgraded firms with an above-average corporate social performance as being a threat to the firm's financial performance. It is typical for the already presented qualitative dichotomy in Sect. 2.1 that for a long time, financial markets have ignored the modernized understanding of a firm's economic role and the relevance of dynamics. With the *knowledge-based theory of the firm*, the real sector adopted a paradigm for the economic understanding of a firm's value crating process, and this adoption is also of relevance for the understanding of the role of CSR and sustainability in the network of a firm with its stakeholders and NGOs.

In the knowledge-based theory of the firm, reputation (among others) is understood as a strategic resource and a dynamic capability in a firm's value creation process in an uncertain and turbulent environment (Völker and Schäfer 2018). To anticipate developments with strategic relevance and an active management of a

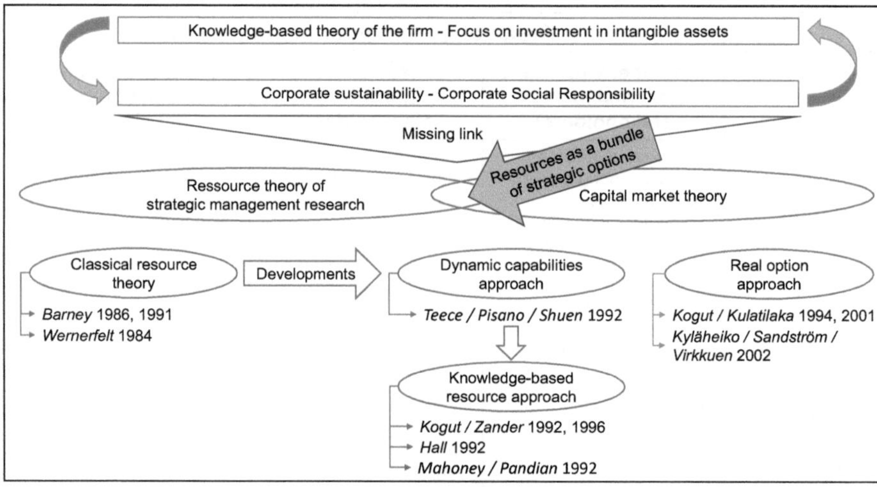

Fig. 5.2 The missing link between value creation and strategic resources as a driver for a firm's acceptance of CSR

firm's *strategic resource base* counts today for most successful firms. Figure 5.2 illustrates an overview of the dynamic capabilities of firms and its development out of the neoclassical resource-based view. Installing and maintaining organizational arrangements to which networking with strategic partners, e.g., NGOs count, allow a firm to operate with *managerial flexibility*. Such a strategic flexibility requires foregoing *investments in dynamic capabilities*, which are commonly understood as investing in *real options* (Schäfer and Sörensen 2010).

There have been various attempts in academic literature to combine the real options approach with the concepts of organizational resources and capabilities. The link can be traced to *Penrose* (1959) who conceptualizes an organization as a device for generating options by distinguishing between an *organization's resources* and the *services* these *resources* can *render*. This view increases the multiple alternative uses for an organization's collection of resources if the knowledge in an organization process increases. Resources hence can contain a "bundle of options" for future strategic choice (Bowman and Hurry 1993, p. 762), which arises through the interaction of the organization's current investments, knowledge, and capacities (Myers 1977). Of main interest for the strategic position of a firm are collaborations that create *tacit knowledge* and investments in such collaborations can be qualified as idiosyncratic (Conner and Prahalad 1996, p. 477). Such knowledge and capacities can stem out the firm itself but also from outside from network partners and even from stakeholders and NGOs. In order to link future organizational capabilities with its future uncertain environment, *Kogut* and *Kulatilaka* (2001, pp. 745, 756) consider the real options approach as a *heuristic framework* to identify and value organizational capabilities. They divided the value of an organization into the present value of its constituent parts and the combinative potential of deploying its capabilities for innovation in existing or new markets.

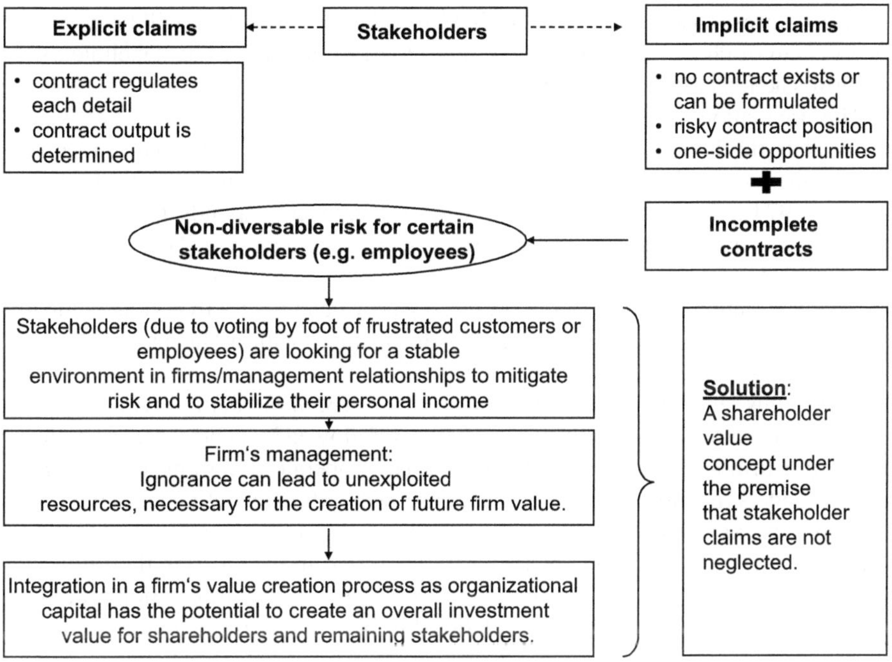

Fig. 5.3 Stakeholder relationships in the context of the contract theory

As will be demonstrated in the next section, CSR and sustainability issues allow a firm to create managerial flexibility as a strategic resource with the character of a real option. A firm's investments in *CSR* and *sustainability* can create *strategic resources* that often would be *intangible* (Atkinson et al. 1997, p. 25) and result from a nexus of contracts with stakeholders and NGOs. This approach offers insights, why contractual relationships of a firm can underlie an economic incentive. To know such a calculus of firms allows stakeholders and NGOs to play a critical role in the enforcement of the license to operate or the license to cooperate (Fombrum et al. 2000).

5.2 Stakeholder Theory, Firm Behavior, and the Link to Finance

From a *normative economic point of view*, CSR could be understood as a way of implementing a fair internalization of negative external effects caused by a firm's economic activities. It would be a way of avoiding negative external effects or compensating the welfare losses of a *firm's external stakeholders*. Figure 5.3 repeats the basics from *contract theory* in stakeholder relationships. It follows the understanding of the instrumental stakeholder theory that addresses issues of sustainability and firm success (Samuelson 1971, p. 24).[1] It is the idea that a firm will be governed by a system of checks and balances in order to avoid any losses to stakeholders by the firm's actions (Monks and Minow 1995).

The orientation of CSR towards *critical stakeholders* affected by a firm's economic activities is essential (Zadek 2004). In addition, certain stakeholders receive a share in the profits of the positive side effects of a firm's economic activity (Eells and Walton 1974). The understanding of CSR strongly corresponds to demands of NGOs that firms should care about their societal responsibilities. Generally speaking, in a global environment with firms' borderless activities, the governance vacuum that national governments are faced with when they try to regulate globally operating firms needs to replace the "law to operate" with a "license to operate" (Reed 2001, p. 14).

Due to this legal prerequisite and the capacity of *shareholders* to *reduce agency costs*, they became the *dominating stakeholders*, followed by debtholders as both are greasing a firm's value chain with money. They operate according to the capital market models mentioned above and are obsessed with the strict quantitative trade-off between expected risk and return. As these models are commonly judged as (ethical) value-free, shareholders are solely interested in maximizing their utility in the *Fisherian* sense, i.e., their income stems from the firm's value creation process in financial terms. For a long time, a relationship between *fairness*, *operational efficiency*, and *goal setting* was *denied*. However, conflicts of interests between the two groups often occur: shareholders maximize their private income, e.g., dividends, and other stakeholders pay the bill (fired workers, bank crisis management at the expense of taxpayers, customers facing low service levels, etc.). Profit maximization in the shareholder value paradigm was often understood as the ignorance of internalizing negative external (social and environmental) costs and underestimated the significance of stakeholders and social capital for a firm's value creation process.

For a long time, the notion of an ethical value-free profit-generating system fitted well with the *benign neglect of external negative effects* in the economic activities of firms and their output. Managers were expected to act as agents for the financial goals of their shareholders, disregarding the interests of third parties (apart from stakeholders) and *not to worry about (negative) external effects.*[2] At the time such managerial thinking in terms of principals and agents often referred to *Friedman* (1962, 1970) who was not only worried about agency costs being incurred but also

---

[1]Besides instrumental stakeholder theory, *Donaldson and Preston (*1995*)* distinguished between *descriptive stakeholder theory* that reflects the actual firm behavior and management's practices and the normative stakeholder theory. The latter one goes beyond the purely economic role of stakeholders in business and states what firms should do to achieve and to maintain appropriate ethical behavior in society. The normative approach has strong ties to philosophical standards and ethics as *Schwartz* and *Saiia* (2012, p. 212) argue: "It should comply with core values, utilitarianism, Kantianism, moral rights, justice and fairness."

[2]More than 30 years later, the most famous proponent of the shareholder value approach, *Rappaport* (2006, p. 237), came to a somewhat different conclusion: "Management's responsibility (. . .) is to pursue long-term value maximization."

afraid of a *discomposed social freedom* if socially responsible managers would interfere in the labor division between the public and private sectors. On the other hand, later works like that of *Pava* and *Krausz* proved that additional costs for a firm caused by social or environmental activities would not automatically lead to a firm's inferior financial performance (Pava and Krausz 1996).

Thinking in terms of *neoliberal economists* like *Friedman* implicitly adheres to *teleological ethics*, especially *utilitarianism*, and has close ties to capital markets. Stock exchange listed and manager-led firms are the points of reference. In fact, non-listed firms seemed to be better described in their economic mission in the way *Bowen* (1953, p. 6) stated earlier: "(. . .) it refers to the obligations of businessmen to pursue those politics, to make those decisions, or to follow those lines of actions which are desirable in terms of the objectives and values of society." Several authors (e.g., McGuire 1963) followed this line of argument and transferred the metaphor of the *businessman* to manager-led firms. It was *Freeman* who made the point about stakeholders that new target groups apart from shareholders might affect business objectives and are critical for a firm's financial success (Freeman 1984). In their model *Cornell* and *Shapiro* (1987) demonstrated how a stakeholder's influence could be integrated into the financing conditions of a firm. The discussion about the role and the impact of stakeholders paved a path to sustainability that, nowadays, is dominating academic discussions and efforts in practice: the responsibility of a firm, i.e., its management is to enable and provide for a socially and ecologically liveable environment.

5.3 Interactions Between Firms, Stakeholder, and Nongovernmental Organizations

In a globalized world with highly mobile capital, firms have incentives to circumvent national regulations that would otherwise impose taxes and statutory requirements, e.g., to internalize negative external effects. Under the regime of a political government, stakeholders can gain a strategic position in the process of finding a pareto-like optimum between market parties and those outside markets. A *governance vacuum* does not automatically imply a societal vacuum as the opposite can in fact be true; it stresses the role of *private initiatives in a civil society*. If government-based mandatory regulations cannot be explicitly or completely formulated, contract theory argues that stakeholders, often in accordance with NGOs and firms, can build up a self-contained uncodified network of relationships (Waddock 2009, p. 71). As, in most cases, the formulation of explicit and complete contracts is impeded by prohibitive transaction costs, such a network would consist of *implicit and incomplete contracts* that cannot be enforced in the courts.

Under those circumstances, the network between contract partners generates *asymmetric information distributions* that can motivate *opportunistic behavior* (e.g., holdup, moral hazard) on the better-informed side of the partnership and

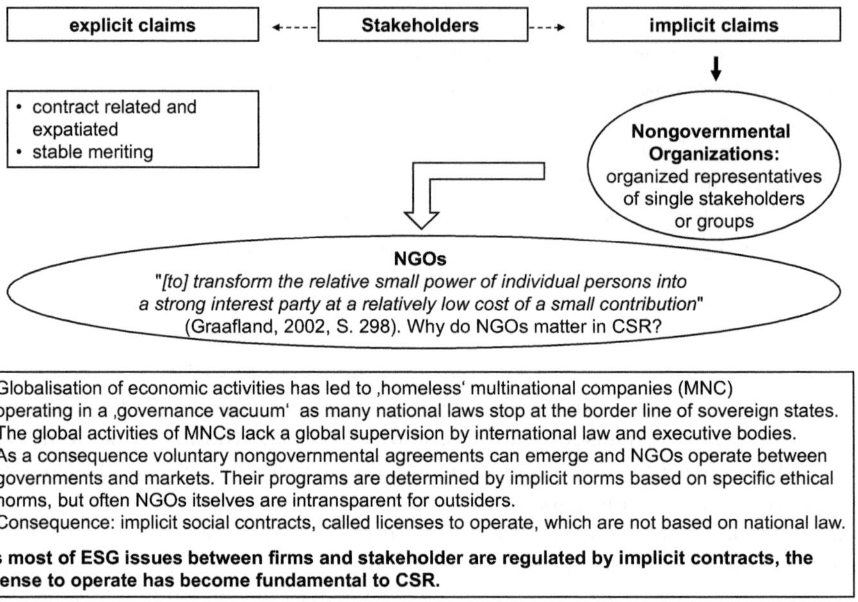

Fig. 5.4 CSR as a response to stakeholder demands in order to maintain a firm's license to operate

makes the contract relationship fragile. Only if the parties had a trustful partnership, which operated constructively and transparently, would the relationship work well and survive. On the other hand, a permanent threat, especially for a firm, could be that an NGO or a stakeholder group could cancel their partnership. Along with the risk that in such a case confidential information from such a broken contract relationship could become public would the firm be prompted to act in a NGO friendly manner, i.e., follows their understanding of a sustainable or responsible business path. Therefore such NGO-based relationships often can be described as a *coalition of threat and merit* in which the *reward-benefit principle* could function.

In addition, as *Cornell* and *Shapiro* (1987) have underlined, it is about behavioral uncertainty which cannot be diversified by a firm (and on the other hand, stakeholders face behavioral uncertainties caused by firms that stakeholders cannot diversify)· This might appear as an incentive for a firm's well-behaving with respect to CSR (see Fig. 5.4).

The *motivations of stakeholders* to act partly *as substitutes or quasi-complementary entities* for governments might be caused by ethical considerations and the consciousness of being active members of the civil society or through governmental backing provided that provisions and supports are offered that ease the stakeholders' organization and operations (Cornell and Shapiro 1987). If stakeholders have adequate means, strategies, and operations at their disposal, they are able to threaten a *firm's resource base*. For years, many events of *NGO activism* about *controversial issues* have illustrated such *civil society power*. They often package the interests and demands of many different single stakeholders together with their bureaucratic interests (like, e.g., maximizing the volume of an NGO's raised monetary funds).[3] According to the logic of market economics, unfriendly attacks from NGOs would aim to *increase* either the *cost function of a firm* or to *undermine future sales revenues*. In either case, the overall resulting effect would be a decline in profits and shareholder value.[4] The outcome of such stakeholder-induced economic burdens on firms would have a comparable effect to a *Pigou* tax or the purchase of an entitlement in the *Coase* manner (Branco and Rodrigues 2007). To avoid such restrictions on their businesses and profits, firms would have an incentive to stop destroying the environment, etc. or to let stakeholders participate in the benefits due to the extraordinary sales revenues and profit margins that would last provided the negative external effects were not internalized (Eells and Walton 1974).

Another way is a variation of the market driven *Coase* model. If markets cannot be opened up due to prohibitive transaction costs, stakeholders could attempt to collaborate with firms to bargain for *soft laws*, like the UN Global Compact (Vogel 2010, pp. 68–70). As argued in the preceding section, hard laws are embedded in a national legal system. Its impact would be extinguished if firms had the opportunity to relocate their activities in regions with more easygoing regulations. Such *regulation arbitrage* and the *limited impact of national laws* could be counterbalanced by stakeholder activities. As the organizational capability of such civil society entities would count most to ensuring their success, globally operating, often networking, and well-organized NGOs might be the best suited to *acting between markets and governments*. NGOs "[to] transform the relative small power of individual persons into a strong interest party at a relatively low cost of a small contribution" (Graafland 2002, p. 298).

Under these circumstances, NGOs would not rely on laws to operate as governments do when they want to get firms on their CSR track. Instead, NGOs presume that they are in the possession of a license that allows firms to cooperate with the NGO. Such *licenses* are *implicit* and *incomplete contractual arrangements*. They are self-constituted by an NGO as they aim to put pressure on a firm if it does not operate in compliance with a NGO's demands. The threat is the danger of *depreciation of mostly intangible* (social, organizational, and human) capital, foremost the damage of a firm's reputation brought about by an NGO's denunciation in the media, in their campaigning and by whistle blowing (Howard-Grenville et al. 2008, p. 77). As *Graafland* (2002, p. 297) explains: "[. . .] the firm will have to take some minimum social responsibility in order to get a license to operate." NGOs absorb, filter, and channel societal expectations concerning the sustainable development and CSR of firms. They try to pressurize firms into demonstrating and deepening their commitment to sustainability and responsibility. It is a precondition to maintaining their *license to operate*. Firms have been learning their lessons and increasingly accepting

---

[3]Related items to the license to operate are social license and social license to operate (Post 2000, p. 36, Reed 2001, p. 14).

[4]Legendary is the "Brent Spar case" (Greenpeace against Royal Dutch Shell) in the 1980s.

that financial success without demonstrable contributions to the public is no longer a viable, long-term strategy. *Waddock* and *Graves* (1997, pp. 306–307) called such an approach in economics *Good Management Theory*.

Apart from NGOs and stakeholders, *share- and bondholders*, in general, represent an *outstanding group of stakeholders*. In a monetary economy, they are responsible for providing funds to firms without which they would be unable to operate. Although the partnership between those financial stakeholders and management is usually based on very explicit contracts, implicit and incomplete parts nevertheless remain. They have inspired huge literary and academic research on principal agent-related corporate governance subjects. Therefore, today the principal agent theory, together with the property rights approach and information economics as parts of *neo-institutionalism*, inseminated academics and practice successfully. Here the focus is on agency costs, the opportunistic behavior of managers as agents, and the designs to reduce a management's discretionary leeway and to bind it to the will and intention of shareholders as principal agents. The discussions about CSR on the firm level are sticking to such paradigms and perceptions.

Traditionally financial stakeholders in their relationships with the management have operated with elements that could be interpreted as a partial license to operate or to cooperate. Today the enforcement of a *sustainable and responsible behavior of firms* in many countries is delegated to *capital markets*. They deliver the measurements with which share- and bondholders attempt to hold firms on a sustainable path or to sanction their deviations from such a path. "Therefore, we will regard SRI as a phenomenon that gradually differs from corporate social responsibility (CSR). More specifically, CSR is directly connected to ethical, environmental, social, and governance practices of the firm, whereas SRI is related to the investors' practices to account for the former" (Scholtens and Sievännen 2012, p. 3). Such strategies are not restricted to capital markets in the narrow sense but encompass all groups of market players. The requirement of a bank which has granted a loan to a firm to get access to unpublished financial data of its customers, the demand of anchor investors to be represented on the advisory board of their investment targets, or the selection of specific collaterals in exchange for the approval of an applied loan are realities in the daily business of banks and other financial intermediaries. Besides the more direct relationships and opportunities for interfering in the daily tasks of the management, capital markets offer platforms for share- and bondholders to interact with a firm's management. According to the principle "one share one vote," holders of ordinary shares have legally documented rights that allow them a variety of *share- and bondholder engagements* towards the *management*. But what makes the difference between such traditional understanding of *corporate governance compared to CSR* and related concepts is the fact that for decades, the subjects of such contractual agreements have been strictly financial. On the other hand, bearing such interactions in mind, one comes closer to the idea of subjugating financial stakeholders for the purposes of CSR. As *Scholtens* (2006, p. 26) pointed out, SRI is a way of pressurizing firms toward CSR-friendly business.

Chapter 6
Concluding Remarks

Abstract Despite the aforementioned potentials of a convergence of ethics and finance, severe obstacles need to be acknowledged and will be discussed in this chapter. In the first part, the main findings of the previous elaborations are recapitulated and summarized. A critical review of common positions in the narrower as well as the wider understanding of sustainability and corporate social responsibility follows. The one-sided view of only negative external effects needs special attention, as free-riding problems can occur whenever the positive external effects of a firm's conduct are overlooked. In addition the contributions of private households internalizing the negative external effects of their individual consumption require attention. Controversial areas of current discussions in sustainable finance are the shortcomings arising from the classification of "good" and "bad" investment targets, the still dominant role of financial performance within investment decisions, the role of financial intermediaries in their role as sustainability accountants and monitors as financial regulators stress it, the information overload of investors together with as yet the unspecific mental drivers of ethics in individual investment decisions, and the underestimated problem of money laundering for ethics in finance.

Keywords Sustainable finance · Socially responsible investments · External effects · Rebound effects · Neuroeconomics · Information overload · Money laundering · Financial regulation

Financial and ethical values seem to matter. It has been the idea of the preceding chapters to discuss *finance* and *ethics* as a kind of *twins*. The first part of the book demonstrated that finance had turned away from a former corporate finance orientation with strong ties to real sector business toward capital market-based approaches that inspired *self-interested, profit-seeking rational investors*. It was demonstrated that the neoclassical approach of *dichotomy*, i.e., the separation of an economic system into a real and a monetary part on the one hand side, served as a useful way to explore the complexity of economic systems (quantitative dichotomy) but on the other hand lead to an ongoing separation in the minds of researcher and practitioners (qualitative dichotomy). This situation is accompanied by influential academic

H. Schäfer, *On Values in Finance and Ethics*, SpringerBriefs in Finance,
https://doi.org/10.1007/978-3-030-04684-2_6

research that developed the tools and generated the data needed to prepare rational investment decisions with a *focus* solely on *monetary values*.

The rising *instability of capital markets* since the breakdown of the *Bretton Woods* world monetary system in the 1970s exponentially increased the need for risk management models and tools. The *capability of* correct *forecasts* of market prices became a historically high awareness among market participants. They were suddenly in heavy need of *sophisticated risk management instruments* employing high-level mathematics, neural network, genetic algorithm, data visualization, chaos theory, etc. (Sanford 1993). Without the strong grounding of statistics, physics, and mathematics, it would scarcely have been possible to cope with the risk caused by market price fluctuations, credit defaults, and fickle cash flows. For *Irving Fisher*, these developments should had given the satisfaction of having got what he had claimed: *research in finance on eye level with natural sciences*. However as the following years illustrated, such technical innovations need to be accompanied by an infusion of psychology, sociology, and philosophy to which ethics belongs.

Reviewing the past decades, it has become apparent that such an unquestionable *quantum jump in finance* was in some parts at the expense of the former close ties between finance and ethics and morality which have been lost. The same can be said about the risen gap between the real and the financial sector. Today a growing number of practitioners, researcher, politicians, NGOs, and journalists are critically reflecting on the daily business of finance, banking, and asset management. Their questions revolve around the misconduct of single representatives of financial intermediaries, fraudulent behavior, excessive profit seeking, astronomical bonus payments, etc. Furthermore, the entire financial system and their private institutions are accused of having compromised the capitalistic system, destabilizing social life and destroying Nature. The *catalog of accusations is long and manifold*. The "man in the street" looks on blankly at such affairs, feels cheated, and not seldom demands the nationalization or divesture of banks and other financial intermediaries. Last but not least, finance is involved in discussions about the lack of justice and equality, as a few capital market participants make their *extraordinary and exorbitant profits* through financial transactions that scam the rest of society.

Parallel to the dubious mutations in capital markets, finance, and its representatives, outlined here, there is a need for a sustainable development to save the "starship earth." Initiatives taken by the United Nations, global think tanks, responsible entrepreneurs, and NGOs have grown over the years and document the urgent need for an orientation of finance to the sustainability approach. Even national governments have become increasingly aware of the *dimensions of unsustainable production* and *consumption*. The current state of global warming, the irresponsible steady increase in greenhouse gas emissions, and the adverse effects of decades of uncontrolled environmental pollutions are now visible and perceptible. Many studies like the *Stern* reports (2007 and 2009) have qualified the investments and measures for avoiding the prolongation of unsustainable growth. They have estimated the amount of dollars, euros, yens, etc. urgently needed for real investments and came to a decisive conclusion: without the mobilization of huge amounts of private capital to cope with these dramatic problems of the century, the public sector would be hopelessly overchallenged.

With the *Paris agreement* on the reduction of greenhouse gas emissions (COP 21) and the publication of the *17 SDGs*, sustainability has succeeded in appearing on the agendas of reputable and influential institutions, circles, etc. The global political and civil society agendas now demand from the financial sector a much more fundamental devotion to and passion for sustainability and climate change, respectively. It is about a new understanding of the financial system: "A 'green finance system' refers to a series of policies, institutional arrangements and related infrastructure building that, through loans, private equity, issuance of bonds and stocks, insurance and other financial services, steer private funds toward green industry" (Green Finance Task Force 2015, p. 6).

A booming new sustainability industry consisting of consultants, accountants, NGOs, networkers, bloggers, social communities, etc. operates with a *Babylonian confusion of terms*. In the financial sector, buzz words like sustainable finance, green finance, impact investing, blended finance, etc. are examples of a mushrooming taxonomy. However, it increasingly entangles and erodes the willingness of those who wish to do good.

For a long time, the academic community ignored all of the former developments in sustainability evolving among asset managers, institutional investors, etc. *Ethical considerations* in capital market theory and finance were envisaged as *alien*, only able to "bug smart models", and should at best be ignored. However, capital market researchers have a long-standing but quietly held tradition of interacting with and advising practitioners and also of developing workable models. The development of the *Black/Scholes* formula, *Sharpe*'s modeling of the CAPM, and *Ross* arbitrage pricing model are only a few examples that demonstrate the openness of capital market research to requirements in practice and its rewards. On the other hand, capital markets academics have successfully cultivated their own academic business models.[1] No wonder that after *years of neglect* due to missing incentives, capital market research has only recently become aware of the enduring and growing interest in practice to integrate ethical factors. It was no longer advisable for academic business models to lose sight of an accelerating investment process in practice, represented by *socially responsible investments* and related investment approaches.

The most fruitful area of such research work was indeed on investment approaches that integrated environmental, social, governance and sometimes ethical criteria. Since the first empirical work on such issues by *Moskowitz* (1972), a *flood of empirical studies* around the world can be noticed. The most frequently researched question was clearly driven by practice: does an investor win or lose if one integrates

[1]For instance, the *Black/Scholes* option pricing formula was inspired by the expectations of *Fisher Black*, employed in the consulting firm Arthur D. Little Inc., and the assistant professor at the Massachusetts Institute of Technology (MIT), *Myron Scholes*, to develop a tool for the practical use in the daily business with derivatives (Heimer and Arend 2008, p. 11).

social, environmental, governance, or ethical parameters into the investment decision? *Financial performance-related* questions inspired so many studies that currently more than 2000 have been counted and assessed in several meta-studies (e.g., Friede et al. 2015; Revelli and Viviani 2015; Cho 2016). Other areas of research in finance that considered ethical aspects are credit spread analysis, risk models, etc. (Weber et al. 2010). It seems justified to conclude that ethical considerations are no longer aliens in the academic community. On the other hand, one has to confess that so far no scientific revolution in the sense of *Kuhn* can be associated with the development outlined.

It is striking that the majority of models extended by any kind of ethical considerations are directly *focused on* financial performance, i.e., *monetary values*. What is still missing is the virtual ethical dimension of finance and capital markets, i.e., the ethical impact of financial transactions and operations. Although the development of impact investing strategies with microfinance at its spearhead is respectable, *mainstream sustainable investing* still *ignores* the dimension of *ethical values* as an overarching target of investments. One very interesting interrelated approach of ethics, impact, and investing can be seen in the field of *social impact bonds*. Generally speaking, here the financial performance is tied together with the social or environmental output, outcome, or impact of the *bond's proceeds* (Johnson and Lee 2013). Such bonds also reflect the need for a new taxonomy. The term "bond" is misleading as it has nothing in common with conventional (straight) bonds. It is a kind of public-private partnership belonging to the investment category of payment through results contracts and functions so completely different when compared with classical bonds (Sturgess et al. 2011). *Stakeholders* most often play an important role in such *contractual networks*.

Doing good by doing well—or doing well by doing good? Do firms rate better in their sustainability performance due to an outstanding corporate financial performance (CFP), or is it the other way round? Strictly speaking we (still) do not know definitely. And this is only one example of the many existing question marks in the relationship between finance and ethics. Although finance and ethics have drawn closer to each other, *severe challenges remain*, and new ones have evolved. Some of these are sketched in the following.

6.1 Only the Bad Counts

The most important closeness to ethical considerations is the *concept of sustainable development*. In it, the theory of negative external effects plays a pivotal analytical role. Simply speaking, foremost firms (and only sometimes governments) are demanded to *internalize negative external effects*. In most cases, contracts that allow to generate negative external effects do not exist (with the exception of greenhouse gas emission allowances). Market solutions for an internalization often fail, and governmental regulation or NGO activism that threatens a firm's license to operate seems to be the only workable alternative. Contrary to widespread convictions, the concept of negative external effects has some severe *shortcomings* in the fields of *corporate sustainability* and *CSR*:

- The *focus* is *on firms*. However, private households as consumers and the negative external effects they cause are still ignored. One should bear in mind that *private households* are severe polluters (e.g., greenhouse gas emissions due to heating systems or excessive travelings) and are often unwilling to act as responsible consumers in order to give firms reliable signals to produce environmentally friendly or socially responsible products and services. *Pigou* taxes on consumption are in most countries the exception as politicians normally take fright of any strains that put a burden on citizens and could threaten their reelection. One can explain this bias by the *median voter in democratic societies*: according to *politico-economic models*, politicians intend to maximize their votes in elections and strive to satisfy the *median voter* who cast the majority of votes. Therefore governments prefer *nudgings* and *moral suasions* to direct private households to a sustainable behavior. Strong *legal duties* are imposed *on firms*, as they have no voting rights in democratic systems. To date no research exists concerning the aforementioned aspects.

  Despite moral suasions and nudgings, consumers in general are still under-exploiting their market power to sanction firms for their ethical violations. An obvious example is the way consumers tackle *corporate governance*. The fraudulent behavior of the German Volkswagen Group ("Dieselgate") since 2015 is an intriguing illustration of opportunistic and irresponsible consumer behavior. The 2017 all-time high annual turnover of the automobile group can be interpreted as a collapse of the often-assigned role of consumers as critical stakeholders who punish unsocial firms through voting by foot. It seems that politicians and public authorities should be very careful in their assumptions about a general "goodness" of consumers. *Hedonistic and egoistic behavior* seems underestimated as main driver for the consumption of the majority of private households. Perhaps it suppresses actions to do good for others and Nature.
- The approach of external effects focuses on the dark side of a firm's economic behavior. What are often overseen are the *positive external effects* of firms. Voluntary social benefits, a responsible utilization of natural resources or a responsible corporate governance, are not marketable, have no market price, and are therefore consumed free of charge by beneficiaries such as communities or stakeholders (free-riding problem). However, this is usually ignored in discussions about integrating ethics into finance. A fair discussion of business ethics should also consider the positive voluntary contributions or by-products of firms on social and environmental issues. In many cases *family-run firms* represent such contributors, but they are set back in the public awareness by the dominance of stock market listed large capitalized companies (Schäfer and Goldschmidt 2010). Undoubtedly, such "large caps" often represent the prototype of a globally operating firm that damages the environment and harms social relationships (e.g., the "Deepwater Horizon" case of BP or violations of human rights of native people in Nigeria by oil drilling operations of Shell). But there exists also a good

side of external effects of firms that should be integrated into discussions of sustainable firm behavior.

6.2 Inside Out and Outside In

Very prominently represented by the SDGs, the sustainable development approach currently focuses on the negative impact of economic transactions and value chains inside production plants, service establishments, networks, etc. on external stakeholders, the Nature, etc. The damaging of such areas should be reduced and at best completely avoided. According to *Denis Meadows* of the Club of Rome think tank, it must be recognized that sustainable contributions neglected in the past have caused massive substantial negative feedbacks on a firm's value chain and private households' living conditions (*rebound effects*). Mitigation and adaptation in the greenhouse gas debate illustrate this. Besides the ethical understanding according to the sustainable development approach, the "Gestalt" of *resilience* becomes relevant and creates a *new interpretation of sustainability and ethics*: the need to protect from the negative rebounds of an unsustainable development. Due to the undeniable threats of global warming resulting in extreme weather events that causes severe damages, ethical considerations in finance should shift to the question of how finance can support an economy and society to become more resilient, i.e., to manage the adverse effects of the unsustainable actions of the past. Such a discussion is still not widespread and should urgently attract greater attention.

6.3 Shades of Gray

More simply one can say that *ethics* is thinking about *what is good and what is bad*. As demonstrated in the preceding chapters, ethics is not a fixed monolith, but requires a permanent discourse, allowing differing positions and changes over time. For many people in industrialized countries, a unique and predominant institution that defines generally accepted moral and ethical positions does not exist anymore. *Ethics and morality have been privatized*. Beyond a (hopefully) unique set of ethical positions, it is up to everyone's individual attitude to define what is right and what is wrong. Differing ethical positions would be reflected in *differing utility functions* and could conflict with the common understanding about value in economics, i.e., the monetary value. Under those circumstances, the allocation of goods and resources would tend to be much more complex and complicated and could lead to suboptimal results in a pure economic sense. *Sandberg* et al. (2009, pp. 529–531) revealed that due to *cultural*, *ethical*, and *regional differences* among investors from different countries, their requirements for an ethical investment deviate remarkable and require different SRI products and strategies. Such challenges also can be found among single investors and groups: fundamental Christians, for instance, ask themselves which industrial sector and which single firm they can invest in. The *exclusion* of so-called *sin stocks* is the classical way of coping with this difficulty (Sparkes and Cowton 2004). But what is sinful? Is it about an all-or-nothing affair or are thresholds allowed (e.g., firms with a weapon producing affiliated company can be invested in if their stake is below 5%), who is legitimized to set the rules? Can it be determined beyond doubt what a negative external effect in a firm's activity means to stakeholders (e.g., does withdrawing an investment from a firm operating with child labor harm the livelihood of the child's family)? There are so many more related questions that demonstrate that the determination of ethical clear-cut positions is often wishful thinking.

6.4 Bringing Home the Bacon

In mainstream finance, ethical considerations have found their role but have to compete with the performance of conventional asset allocations that operate without ESG parameters. "In this mainstreamable form of RI [Responsible Investment, H. Schäfer], ESG issues could be considered only in so far as they might be financially material and no further. There was no room in this for constraining individual greed (...)" (Eccles 2011, p. 26). Such an *absence of a deontological ethical motivation* in SRI means that investors expect from the integration of ESG criteria in their investment decisions a *superior return/risk relationship*, i.e., a financial outperformance. Indeed many empirical works have found evidences that no underperformance of SRI portfolios compared to conventional ones exist (Schröder 2014). From a *teleological ethical point* of view, SRI could deliver instruments to control and sanction investees with respect to a sustainable behavior. The *impact investing* and *thematic investing* approaches have evolved with such a motivation. These approaches are much more project related and link the real positive social output, outcome, or impact of a financed project to its financial return. At first glance, such an investment approach fascinates by its very ethical nature, but a closer look reveals that even here investors with *risk/return priorities dominate* (Eckert and Schäfer 2014). This raises the question, whether investments with real and sustainable social improvements by their positive external effects really can be achieved by private investors.

6.5 Setting a Fox to Keep the Geese

The Financial Stability Board's Task Force on Climate-Related Financial Disclosures (TCFD) (2016), the initiative of the UNEP (2015), the European Commission (2018), and many central banks are convinced that the *banking sector* has to play the *major role* in the *transmission to a sustainable* (or green) *economy* and society. The idea is striking as *monetary economies* cannot exist without a functioning financial sector. In some countries, such a sector is dominated by banks (e.g., in Germany, Japan); other countries with their particular financial ecosystem are more reliant on capital markets (Jeucken 2004, p. 122). The *pivotal role* that *money* plays in economic transactions has already been discussed at the beginning of the book. The subprime and banking crises and many other previous crises have demonstrated the importance of a functioning and efficient financial sector for the sake of the welfare of societies. Official authorities would be well advised to keep their eye on banks, institutional investors, capital markets, etc. A somewhat strange idea is currently circulating in international and supranational organizations that moves financial intermediaries to the frontline of the struggle against greenhouse gas emissions and global warming.

Although national climate action plans according to the *COP 21* agreement have defined reduction goals only for nonfinancial sectors, banks and others should operate as enablers of adaptation and mitigation (Schäfer 2018). The clue is seen in the phenomenon of *financed emissions* (UNEP FI 2013). Currently, this seems to be one of the most dazzling and misunderstood terms. According to the Greenhouse Gas Protocol (2013) and its *Scope 3 classification*, financial intermediaries should decide which investment, loan, or any other financial transaction can be accepted as climate-friendly and which has to be rejected (so-called financed emissions). In the aftermath of the subprime and banking crises, banks and other financial institutions have been blamed for their unreliability and irresponsibility. So the idea that they should serve as guarantors of a turnaround in climate change-related economic activities of nonfinancial sectors is fanciful. It is questionable how the focus of the regulators on climate change can be justified compared to many and many more relevant threats to the stability of the financial sector like jeopardizing *credit pyramiding*, *shadow banks*, and the *too netted to fail* problem—to mention only a few.

6.6 It Is Always Good to Be Good

Decades after ignorance of intensified discussions among politicians, managers, NGOs, and media, academic research has approached to tackle generally speaking "nonfinancial issues." Herein, environmental, social, and much more governance issues have entered capital market models, business models, and management approaches. Supported by the United Nations Environment Program, new research think tanks like the PRI Academy, reputable university-based research institutions, and research circles have evolved. Indeed, it seems that after years of ignorance and partly refusal by the academic community, sustainability and CSR issues have conquered research agendas. Despite this growing awareness, it is remarkable that such research seems to follow a biased trend. For instance, most empirical studies confirm that CSR has a positive correlation to corporate financial performance. Such findings and others seem to reflect a *generally positive attitude of researchers* against CSR-related subjects. *Rost* and *Ehrmann* (2015) have identified in their meta-study of existing empirical studies that many of them are biased by a *value judgment*, i.e., a predetermined positive attitude of research concerning CSR and sustainability. Critical reflections and in such a way helpful inspirations for practitioners seem to be exceptional.

6.7 Power to the People

The integration of ethical considerations in general and sustainable issues in particular rests on the fundamental pillar of the existence of an *ethical goodwill among people*. The argument that firms, governments, and any other investing entities ought to operate in harmony with Nature and provide social well-being is ultimately grounded on the assumption of the existence of a general consensus among and willingness of stakeholders concerning ethics and morality. A closer look at *different stakeholder groups*, self-declared representatives, and *NGOs* reveals a somewhat different picture. As already mentioned in Sect. 6.1, great hopes in democratic societies and market economies rest on consumers. In principle they can translate their ethical concerns by means of buying products for their positive ethical qualities or by boycotting products for their negative qualities. However, surveys among customers and with different research topics demonstrate a *discrepancy between attitudes and ethical buying behavior*: private households utter a high willingness to pay a higher price for sustainable products, but the market share of such products still remains low (Pelsmacker et al. 2005, pp. 363–365). In addition, repeated cross-national surveys among retail customers about their *willingness to pay* for a sustainable product (see Fig. 6.1 and cited source) exhibit the problem of "being concerned (about environmental and social problems) but not willing to act" (to pay a higher price for sustainable products).

Besides the *consumption problem,* other areas of *private households' contributions to sustainability* like the decreasing willingness to reduce or separate waste; the severe increase of greenhouse gas emissions, e.g., due to the boom in air travel; the reluctance to engage in electromobility; etc. actually do not prove a high degree of awareness and responsibility among consumers. Comparable *shortcomings* can be observed concerning sustainable investments. An outline of challenges to understand the behavior of ethically minded investors is worthwhile. Currently, available research evidence indicates a variety of *biases* among private household investors that contradict the assumption of purely rational investment decision-making, mainly in the field of sustainable investments. Research findings and practitioners' experiences in SRI and impact investing highlight a much greater relevance of *behavioral finance* in explaining investor decisions. The most frequently identified causes are *home biases*, *overoptimism*, *overconfidence*, *social infection and imitation*, etc. Such observations suggest an extraordinary relevance of rules of thumb, emotional influences, and other nonrational criteria for decision-making among sustainable-minded investors (Godeke et al. 2009; Eckert and Schäfer 2014). With reference to fundamental economic theory, situations in which an individual chooses

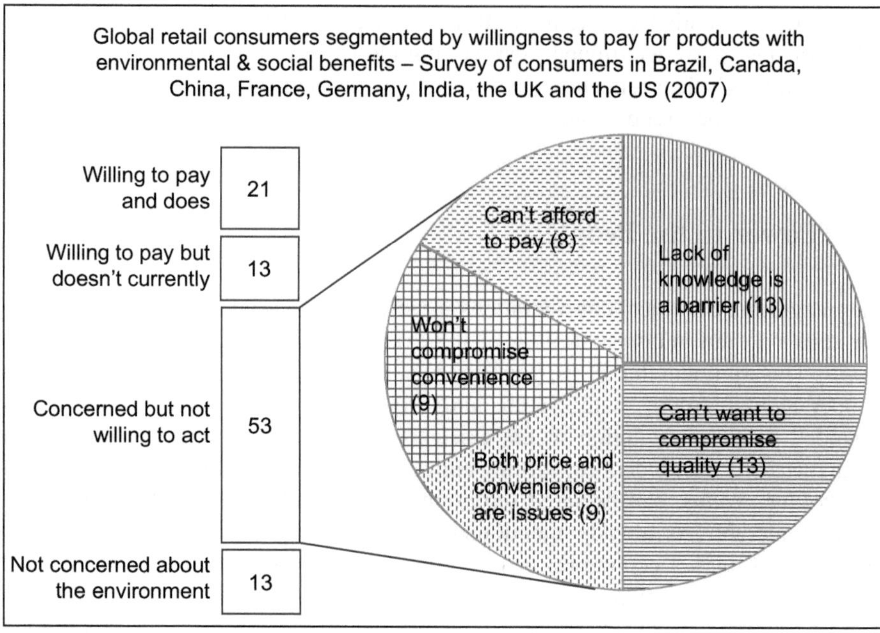

Fig. 6.1 The challenge for stakeholder in consumption (Bonini et al. 2008, p. 8)

a suboptimal alternative that reaches or surpasses an aspiration level have come to be known as *satisficing* (Simon 1955). Perhaps in the area of sustainable investments, such a *bounded rationality* is a more appropriate description of investment decisions than for strictly financially based decision-makings. It would be rewarding to explore in more detail how the behavioral considerations for investment decisions among ethically minded investors can be explained—not only to fill an academic gap in research but also to assist practitioners in their daily business.

6.8 "Brain Salad Surgery"

It is a commonly held belief in capital market theory that the usefulness for a sustainable-minded investor is derived from the financial outcome of the investment and the benefits from the ecological and social outcome or impact of that investment (Dorfleitner and Nguyen 2017). The mathematical modeling of an ethically minded investor's objective is somewhat problematic (Hallerbach et al. 2004). It raises the difficulty of trying to measure the degree to which environmental, social, and governance issues are integrated into any individual investment decision, since this is no welfare function that includes all social aspects and rates of trade-off between them. If one takes *individual utility with subjective ethical values* into account, an interesting approach to measuring the utility of ethically related decisions is indicated by a new research branch of economics, i.e., *neuroeconomics*. Initial applications of neuroeconomic techniques in the fields of environmentally related economic decision-making show new findings that could differ from prevailing research agendas in sustainable finance (Glimcher et al. 2016). "The results show that neural activity associated with the subjective valuation of environmental proposals differs profoundly from the neural activity associated with previously examined goods and preference measures" (Khaw et al. 2015, p. 1). It seems that further research based on neuroeconomic approaches might deepen and broaden the understanding of investment decisions based on ethical considerations and subjective ethical values. Perhaps such approaches have the potential to shed a somewhat different light on our current understanding of an efficient asset allocation with respect to ESG criteria.

6.9 Information Overflow

Sustainable investments require asset allocation strategies that integrate sustainability, i.e., *extra-financial data*. Such ESG data is then the complement to state-of-the-art financial key performance indicators. As *nonfinancial data*, they are interpreted in mainstream economics as additional information that can be exploited in order to improve an investment portfolio's risk-return profile or to align a portfolio with certain organizational values. The nature of additionality leads to a variety of challenges for managers of sustainable investment portfolios, individual investors, etc. in processing the information with regard to *quantity*, *quality*, and *complexity* (Hafenstein and Bassen 2016; Reimsbach et al. 2017). These three factors contribute to *information overload*.

Research has found a number of *negative consequences* for when information overload exceeds an *information-processing capacity*. It may lead to lower performance in complex tasks, to less systematic and less thorough search strategies in the case of capital budgeting (Swain and Haka 2000), to a diminution in decision performance in the context of financial distress (Ding and Beaulieu 2011), and to lower predictive accuracy in the case of financial analysis (Simnett 1996). An *accelerating problem* of information overload is its combination with low *financial literacy*. Many studies document a generally low financial literacy in average private households in many countries concerning basic investment subjects like retirement provision, risk-adjusted investing, indebtedness, etc. (Lusardi and Tufano 2009; Mason and Wilson 2000). Sustainable investment decisions in private households might be further complicated by an information overflow in combination with a low financial capability and a bounded rationality (Beal et al. 2005, p. 66ff.). If such a situation were widespread among private households, not only might their individual wealth positions tend to be inefficient, but one also should expect a low capability of these investors to influence the behavior of investees towards a more ethical business path. Under those circumstances, many *private households* easily could be *overstrained* with a role that NGOs, politicians, and governments like to attribute private households as prudent investors and responsible stakeholders.

6.10 A Wolf in Sheep's Clothing?

Generally speaking, sustainable finance and investments in particular is about the question: *Where does the money go?* As demonstrated in the preceding chapters, the basic idea is that investors worry about output, outcome, or impact of their investment decisions with respect to positive ESG effects (or the avoidance of negative effects on such issues). From an academic point of view, it is about the *external effects of money* in economic transactions as a mean of exchange, a store of wealth, and a unit of account. With these attributes the economic role of money follows the conventional understanding as it was explored in the microeconomic theory of money and the theory of banking (see Sect. 2.1). However, what is left out in these approaches is the role of money as a *medium of anonymization*. The veiling of the origin of actions behind money and monetized transactions allows the turn from good money into "*dirty money*" as *Schneider* (2002, p. 6) has described it. By focusing on the direction of invested money, academics and practitioners do not keep an eye on the other side of the coin, i.e., the question: *Where does the money come from?*

In the last decades, governments of many OECD countries have launched legal acts to combat *money laundering*. They also have installed corresponding regulations on banking and on financial markets as well. However, money laundering and related subjects are still topics on international agendas like the G20 and G7 summits. There is no doubt that money laundering is the ugly face of unethical and unmoral economic transactions. The reasons lie in the illegal and illegitimate actions that ground money laundering as they stem from shadow economies, terror financing, tax frauds, and criminal offenses. Despite efforts of governments to dry out illicit financial flows, *Unger* (2013) proofed that money laundering is still on a steady increase. *Schneider* and *Caruso* (2011) give an illustrative description of the manifold sources of illegal funds. They also highlight the role of charities, ethnical communities, and religious foundations as important entities that allocate illegal funds. *Schneider* (2013) argues that illegal cross-border flows of global "dirty money" have by far reached the biggest share of all illegal transactions. He also found proofs that *transnational organized crime* (TOC) infiltrates official economic systems and that banking and financial centers still play a crucial in this process.

Under those circumstances, the relationship of finance and ethics ought to be completed by the investigation into *money's dark sources*. A still unresolved and to our best knowledge not even posed question ought to be investigated in the near future: Does the mentioned infiltration of the official economic system by TOC threatens SRI and other sustainable finance activities as possible money laundering channels ("the greening of dirty money")? This question seems of relevance as the SDG no. 16 (peace, justice, and strong institutions) with its regarding indicators 16.4

(reduce illicit financial and arms flows) and 16.5 (substantially reduce corruption and bribery) having been installed to strive for significant reduction of illicit financial flows of TCO and the return of stolen assets to their former owners (Vorrath and Beisheim 2015). Although these references do not link to sustainable finance, measures to meet the target cannot ignore or circumvent the "*dark side of finance*."

Chapter 7
Perspectives

Abstract The elaboration on finance and ethics finishes by highlighting the indistinguishable convergence of these two areas in practice and the still retained acknowledgements of such a link in the academic world. Once again, the challenges from climate change and the need to contribute to sustainable development are emphasized. If finance and capital markets really are required to contribute to ethical, environmental, social, and governance issues, transparencies, and proofs of the output, outcome and impact of financial transactions are essential. Otherwise sustainable, green, socially responsible or impact finance pay nothing more than lip service and undermine the credibility of actions that promise to be ethical outcomes.

Keywords Impact investing · Climate change sustainable development goals · Investors

The question marks of the preceding chapter should illustrate that *ethics and finance* still have to experience a long way. They are in *partly convergence* and the pathways are promising. It is not ironic to argue that the existence of a severe crisis—climate change and disruption in banking and finance—offers a real opportunity for a reflection of *finance in the house of ethics*. There has been no better time to remember the forgotten trails and to recognize the promising pathways of an integrated ethics in finance. By looking into the practice of asset management, one can confess a growing awareness to integrate ethical, environmental, social, and governance issues into financial analysis and investment decisions. Starting from religious and clerical investors who tried to avoid investments in "sin stocks," sustainable or socially responsible investing has become part of many *institutional investors*. Private household investors have also been infected by the wish to do good for nature and society, but in many countries they lag in their investment volume behind institutional investors. It might happen that the SDGs and COP21 together with upcoming regulations in the European Union and supported by the recommendations of the G20 and the TCFD will push the integration of ESG issues into asset allocations. It can be expected that under the label of *green finance* stress tests, scenario analysis and other recommendations of regulatory authorities will

H. Schäfer, *On Values in Finance and Ethics*, SpringerBriefs in Finance,
https://doi.org/10.1007/978-3-030-04684-2_7

enter the controlling departments of financial intermediaries and become an integral part of the bulk of already existing reportings and supervisions.

On the *academic side*, nonfinancial parameters have found access to state-of-the-art capital market models. The impressive number of empirical contributions on the financial performance of sustainable asset portfolios compared to their conventional counterparts could reduce skepticism about a long-lasting fear among investors to face an underperformance problem when investing sustainably. Although sustainability issues are still neglected in the majority of reputable global academic research, a growing body of researchers accepts the necessity of such a research branch. Beyond the financial aspects of sustainable finance, much interest arises about the output, outcome, and impact of sustainable investing in the real sector and whether investors really can improve living conditions, the environment, etc. or at minimum prevent from further damages. Such *impact proofs* seem *urgently needed*, as the concept of sustainable investments is strongly linked to the hypothesis that financial operations and transactions can be used as a leverage to stimulate and sanction firms, private households, and even governments to follow a sustainable path.

How finance and ethics can come closer together is not yet described in academic research papers, publications, or textbooks. A *useful compass* is needed to find the right path. This is a real challenge for economics in research and practice, but it seems that it is *worth the trouble*. The prospect is clear: if mainstream finance has integrated ethical and ESG issues to be daily business than no one needs to talk about "exotic" *sustainable investments* and *green finance* anymore—the today approaches and their proponents *would then have become obsolete*.

Correction to: Introduction

Correction to:
Chapter 1 in: H. Schäfer, *On Values in Finance and Ethics*, SpringerBriefs in Finance, https://doi.org/10.1007/978-3-030-04684-2_1

The original version of the book was inadvertently published with the incorrect information on page 2.

The text "The holder of the Nobel Prize for economics 1997, *Richard C. Merton*…" has now been corrected to "The holder of the Nobel Prize for economics 1997, ***Robert*** *C. Merton*…".

The updated online version of the chapter can be found at
https://doi.org/10.1007/978-3-030-04684-2_1

H. Schäfer, *On Values in Finance and Ethics*, SpringerBriefs in Finance,
https://doi.org/10.1007/978-3-030-04684-2_8

Bibliography

Alchian AA (1977) Why money? J Money Credit Bank 9:7–16
Alchian A, Allen A (1983) Exchange and production, 3rd edn. Wadsworth, Belmont, CA
Arrow KJ (1964) The role of securities in the optimal allocation of risk-bearing. Rev Econ Stud 31:91–96
Atkinson G (2000) Measuring corporate sustainability. J Environ Plan Manag 43(2):235–252
Atkinson G (2015) Inequality: what can be done. Harvard Business Press, Cambridge, MA
Atkinson G, Waterhouse JH, Wells RB (1997) A stakeholder approach to strategic performance measurement. Sloan Manag Rev 38(3):25–37
Ballestero E, Pérez-Gladish B, Garcia-Bernabeu A (2015) Socially responsible investment – a multi-criteria decision making approach. Springer, Cham
Ban Ki-moon (2012) Remarks to "KPMG Summit: Business Perspective for Sustainable Growth". https://www.un.org/sg/en/content/sg/statement/2012-02-14/remarks-%E2%80%9Ckpmg-summit-business-perspective-sustainable-growth%E2%80%9D. Accessed 4 Aug 2018
Barney JB (1986) Strategic factor markets: expectations, luck and business strategy. Manag Sci 32 (10):1231–1241
Barney JB (1991) Firm resources and sustained competitive advantage. J Manag 17(1):99–120
Baron MW, Pettit P, Slote M (1997) Three methods of ethics: a debate. Blackwell, London
Bartlett RC, Collins SD (2011) Nicomachean ethics. University of Chicago Press, Chicago, IL
Bassiry GR, Jones M (1993) Adam Smith and the ethics of contemporary capitalism. J Bus Ethics 12:621–627
Baumol WJ (1968) On the social rate of discount. Am Econ Rev 58(4):788–802
Beal DJ, Goyen M, Phillips P (2005) Why do we invest ethically? J Invest 14(3):66–77
Beck U (1992) Risk society: towards a new modernity. Sage, New Delhi
Benston GJ, Smith WS (1976) A transaction approach to the theory of financial intermediation. J Financ 31(2):215–231
Bentham J (1789) An introduction to the principles of morals and legislation. London (1970)
Bernstein R (1992) Capital ideas. Free Press, New York
Bernstein P (1996) Against the gods – the remarkable story of risk. Wiley, New York
Berry T, Carson L, White S (2003) We are all stakeholders: participatory decision-making and corporate sustainability. Contribution to the Corporate Social Responsibility & Environment conference, University of Leeds, UK, 30 June–1 July 2003
Besley T, Ghatak M (2007) Retailing public goods: the economics of corporate social responsibility. J Public Econ 91(9):1645–1663
Black F, Scholes M (1973) The pricing of options and corporate liabilities. J Polit Econ 81 (3):637–654

H. Schäfer, *On Values in Finance and Ethics*, SpringerBriefs in Finance,
https://doi.org/10.1007/978-3-030-04684-2

Boatright JR (1999) Ethics in finance. Blackwell, London

Bonini MJ, Hintz G, Mendonca LT (2008) Addressing consumer concerns about climate change. McKinsey Q:1–9. http://www.mckinseyquarterly.com/Strategy/Strategic_Thinking/Addressing_consumer_concerns_about_climate_change_2115. Accessed 25 Aug 2018

Bowen H (1953) Social responsibilities of the businessman. Harper, New York

Bowman EH, Hurry D (1993) Strategy through the option lens: an integrated view of resource investments and the incremental-choice process. Acad Manag Rev 18(4):760–782

Branco M, Rodrigues L (2007) Positioning stakeholder theory within the debate on corporate social responsibility. J Bus Ethics Organ Stud 12(1):5–15

Brav A, Jiang W, Partnoy F, Thomas R (2008) The returns to hedge fund activism. ECGI Law Working Paper No 098/2008. https://www0.gsb.columbia.edu/mygsb/faculty/research/pubfiles/4132/jiang_activism.pdf. Accessed 4 Aug 2018

Brealey RA, Myers SC, Allen F (2011) Principles of corporate finance, 10th edn. McGraw-Hill, New York

Breslau D (2003) Economics invents the economy: mathematics, statistics, and models in the work of Irving Fisher and Wesley Mitchel. Theory Soc 32:379–411

Brunner K, Meltzer AH (1971) The use of money: money in the theory of an exchange economy. Am Econ Rev 61(5):784–805

Buritt R, Schaltegger S (2001) Eco-efficiency in corporate budgeting. https://www.leuphana.de/fileadmin/user_upload/Forschungseinrichtungen/csm/files/Arbeitsberichte_etc/05-4downloadversion.pdf. Accessed 4 Aug 2018

Carroll AB (1999) Corporate social responsibility: evolution of a definitional construct. Bus Soc 38 (3):268–295

Carroll AB, Buchholtz AK (2008) Business and society: ethics and stakeholder management, 7th edn. Cengage Learning, Mason, OH

Cheung SNS (1973) The fable of the bees: an economic investigation. J Law Econ 16(1):11–33

Cho CY (2016) Academic literature on ESG and financial performance. The Michael Lee-Chin Family Institute of Corporate Citizenship, Toronto

Clower RW (1977) The anatomy of monetary theory. Am Econ Rev., Papers & Proceedings 67 (1):206–212

Coase RH (1960) The problem of social cost. J Law Econ 3:1–44

Conner KR, Prahalad CK (1996) A resource-based theory of the firm: knowledge versus opportunism. Organ Sci 7(5):477–501

Copeland TE, Weston JF, Shastri K (2005) Financial theory and corporate policy, 4th edn. Addison-Wesley, Boston, MA

Cornell B, Shapiro AC (1987) Corporate stakeholders and corporate finance. Financ Manag 16 (1):5–14

Cossin D (2009) Financial engineering's fallout. MIT Sloan Manag Rev 50(2):19

Cox JC, Ross SA, Rubinstein M (1979) Option pricing: a simplified approach. J Financ Econ 7 (3):229–263

Creti A, Jouvet PA, Mignon V (2012) Carbon price drivers. Phase I versus phase II equilibrium? Energy Econ 34(1):327–334

Dahlsrud A (2008) How corporate social responsibility is defined: an analysis of 37 definitions. Corp Soc Responsib Environ Manag 15(1):1–13

Dalal-Clayton B (1999) What is sustainable development? http://www.nssd.net/otherdocuments/sustdev2.doc. Accessed 4 Aug 2018

Dallas L (2011) Short-termism, the financial crisis, and corporate governance. J Corp Law 37 (2):264–363

Daly HE (1991) Sustainable development: from conceptual theory towards operational principles. In: Davis K, Bernstam M (eds) Resources, environment, and population: present knowledge, future options. Oxford University Press, Oxford, pp 25–43

Dauten CA (1948) Business finance. Prentice-Hall, Englewood Cliffs, NJ

Dean J (1951) Capital budgeting. Columbia University Press, New York

Debreu G (1959) The theory of value. Wiley, New York

Dewing AS (1920) The financial policy of corporations. Ronald Press, New York
Diamond DW (1984) Financial intermediation and delegated monitoring. Rev Econ Stud 51:393–414
Ding S, Beaulieu P (2011) The role of financial incentives in balanced scorecard-based performance evaluations: correcting mood congruency biases. J Account Res 49(5):1223–1247. https://doi.org/10.1111/j.1475-679X.2011.00421.x
Donaldson T, Preston LE (1995) The stakeholder theory of the corporation. Acad Manag Rev 20 (1):65–91
Donaldson T, Werhane PH (1996) Ethical issues in business. A philosophical approach. Prentice Hall, Upper Saddle River, NJ
Dorfleitner G, Nguyen M (2017) A new approach for optimizing responsible investments dependently on the initial wealth. J Asset Manag 18(2):81–98
Dosi G, Egidi M (1991) Substantive and procedural uncertainty: an exploration of economic behaviours in changing environments. J Evol Econ 1(2):145–168
EC (2011) A renewed EU strategy 2011–2014 for corporate social responsibility. https://eur-lex.europa.eu/LexUriServ/LexUriServ.do?uri=COM:2011:0681:FIN:EN:PDF. Accessed 6 Sept 2018
Eccles N (2011) New values in responsible investment. In: Vandekerckhove W, Leys J, Alm K, Scholtens B, Signore S, Schaefer H (eds) Responsible investments in times of turmoil. Springer, Amsterdam, pp 19–34
Eckert S, Schäfer H (2014) Risk, return... and impact? Current attitudes of selected German investors towards social impact investing. Bertelsmann Foundation. https://www.bertelsmann-stiftung.de/fileadmin/files/user_upload/German_Investor_Attitudes_towards_SII.pdf. Accessed 2 Sept 2018
Eells R, Walton C (1974) Conceptual foundations of business. Richard D. Irwin, Homewood, IL
Elkington J (1998) Cannibals with forks: the triple bottom line of 21st century business. Environ Qual Manag 8(1):37–51
Errico L, Farahbaksh M (1998) Islamic banking: issues in prudential regulations and supervision. IMF Working Paper, No. 30. Monetary and Exchange Affairs Department. http://www.imf.org/external/pubs/ft/wp/wp9830.pdf. Accessed 20 Aug 2018
Etzioni A (1991) Reflections on teaching of business ethics. Bus Ethics Q 1(4):355–365
EU High-Level Expert Group on Sustainable Finance (2018) Financing a sustainable European economy. Brussels. https://ec.europa.eu/info/sites/info/files/180131-sustainable-finance-final-report_en.pdf. Accessed 2 Sept 2018
European Commission (2018) Action plan: financing sustainable growth. https://eur-lex.europa.eu/legal-content/EN/TXT/PDF/?uri=CELEX:52018DC0097&from=EN. Accessed 4 Aug 2018
Fama E (1970) Efficient capital markets. J Financ 25(3):383–417
Fama E (1991) Efficient capital markets: II. J Financ 46(5):1575–1617
Federal Bureau of Investigation (2011) Hedge fund billionaire Raj Rajaratnam found guilty in Manhattan Federal Court of insider trading charges. https://archives.fbi.gov/archives/newyork/press-releases/2011/hedge-fund-billionaire-raj-rajaratnam-found-guilty-in-manhattan-federal-court-of-insider-trading-charges. Accessed 4 Aug 2018
Fisher I (1892) Mathematical investigations in the theory of value and prices, vol 1965. Yale University Press, New Haven, CT
Fisher I (1930) The theory of interest as determined by impatience to spend income and opportunity to invest it. Macmillan, New York
Fombrum CJ, Gardberg NA, Barnett ML (2000) Opportunity platforms and safety nets: corporate citizenship and reputational risk. Bus Soc Rev 105(1):85–106
Freeman RE (1984) Strategic management: a stakeholder approach. Pitman, Boston, MA
Friede G, Busch T, Bassen A (2015) ESG and financial performance: aggregated evidence from more than 2000 empirical studies. J Sustain Financ Invest 5(4):210–233
Friedman M (1953) Essays in positive economics. University of Chicago Press, Chicago, IL
Friedman M (1962) Capitalism and freedom. University of Chicago Press, Chicago, IL

Friedman M (1970) The social responsibility of business is to increase its profits. New York Times Magazine:33

Friedman D (1987) Just price. In: Eatwell J (ed) The new Palgrave, vol 2. Macmillan, London, pp 1043–1044

G20 Green Finance Study Group (2016) G20 green finance synthesis report. https://www.unepinquiry.org/wp-content/.../Synthesis_Report_Full_EN.pdf. Accessed 4 Aug 2018

Garriga E, Melé D (2004) Corporate social responsibility theories: mapping the territory. J Bus Ethics 53:51–71

Giddens A (1998) The third way: the renewal of social democracy. Polity, Cambridge

Glimcher PW, Groswald L, Levinson A, Livermore MA, Macauley MK, Trtanj J (2016) Neuroeconomics: a new direction for valuing environmental public goods. Resources for the Future, Washington, DC. Retrieved from https://youtu.be/N_X9r8wWjFw

Global Reporting Initiative (2015) G4 sustainability reporting guidelines. https://www.globalreporting.org/resourcelibrary/GRIG4-Part1-Reporting-Principles-and-Standard-Disclosures.pdf. Accessed 4 Oct 2018

GLOBESCAN (2017) The 2017 sustainability leaders: celebrating 20 years of leadership. https://globescan.com/wp-content/uploads/2017/07/GSS-Leaders-2017-Survey-Report.pdf. Accessed 4 Aug 2018

GLOBESCAN, BSR (2012) State of sustainable business poll 2012. https://www.bsr.org/en/our-insights/report-view/bsr-globescan-state-of-sustainable-business-poll-2012. Accessed 04 Aug 2018

Godeke S, Pomares R, Bruno AV, Guerra P, Kliessner C, Shefrin H (2009) Solutions for impact investors - from strategy to implementation. Rockefeller Philanthropy Advisors, New York

Graafland JJ (2002) Profits and principles – four perspectives. J Bus Ethics 35(4):293–305

Granger CWJ, Morgenstern O (1970) Predictability of stock market prices. Heath Lexington Booke, Lexington, MA

Green Finance Task Force (2015) Establishing China's green financial system. Final Report of the Green Finance Task Force. Beijing. https://www.cbd.int/financial/privatesector/chinaGreen%20Task%20Force%20Report.pdf. Accessed 14 Sept 2018

Greenbaum S, Hong H, Thakor A (1981) Bank loan commitments and interest rate volatility. J Bank Financ 5(2):497–510

Greenhouse Gas Protocol (2013) Technical guidance for calculating scope 3 emissions – supplement to the corporate value chain (scope 3) accounting & reporting standard. https://www.ghgprotocol.org/sites/default/files/ghgp/standards/Scope3_Calculation_Guidance_0.pdf. Accessed 4 Aug 2018

Gutenberg E (1958) Einführung in die Betriebswirtschaftslehre. Gabler, Wiesbaden

Hafenstein A, Bassen A (2016) Influences for using sustainability information in the investment decision-making of non-professional investors. J Sustain Finance Invest 6(3):186–210. https://doi.org/10.1080/20430795.2016.1203598

Hall R (1992) The strategic analysis of intangible resources. Strateg Manag J 13(2):135–144

Hallerbach W, Ning H, Soppe A, Spronk J (2004) A framework for managing a portfolio of socially responsible investments. Eur J Oper Res 153:517–529. https://doi.org/10.1016/S0377-2217(03)00172-3

Haugen RA (1995) The new finance: the case against efficient markets. Prentice Hall, Englewood Cliffs, NJ

Heimer T, Arend S (2008) The genesis of the Black-Scholes option pricing formula. Frankfurt School – Working Paper Series, No. 98, Frankfurt School of Finance & Management, Frankfurt am Main

Henley N, Spash CL (1993) Cost benefit analysis and the environment. Edward Elgar, Cheltenham

Hirshleifer J (1973) Exchange theory. The missing chapter. West Econ J 11(2):129–146

Hirshleifer J, Riley JG (1979) The analytics of uncertainty and information – an expository survey. J Econ Lit 17(12):1375–1421

Hoagland HE (1933) Corporation finance. McGraw-Hill, New York

Hofstede G (1997) The business of international business is culture. In: Vernon-Wortzel H, Wortzel L (eds) Strategic management in a global economy, 3rd edn. Wiley, Hoboken, NJ, pp 483–493
Hoover KD (1984) Two types of monetarism. J Econ Lit 22:58–76
Hopkins M (1998) A planetary bargain: CSR comes of age. Macmillan, London
Horrigan JO (1987) The ethics of the new finance. J Bus Ethics 6(2):97–110
Howard BB, Upton M (1953) Introduction to business finance. McGraw-Hill, New York
Howard-Grenville J, Nash J, Coglianese C (2008) Constructing the license to operate – internal factors and their influence on corporate environmental decisions. Law Policy 30(1):73–107
IPCC (Intergovernmental Panel on Climate Change) (2007) Climate change 2007 – mitigation of climate change: working group III contribution to the fourth assessment report of the IPCC. Cambridge University Press, New York
Jensen MC, Meckling WH (1976) Theory of the firm: managerial behavior, agency costs, and ownership structure. J Financ Econ 3(2):305–360
Jeucken M (2004) Sustainability in finance: banking on the planet. Eborn Publ, Delft
Johnson K, Lee H (2013) Impact investing: a framework for decision making. Cambridge Associates LLC, Boston, MA
Kahneman D, Tversky A (1979) Prospect theory: an analysis of decision under risk. Econometrica 67(2):263–291
Kant I (1785) Grundlegung zur Metaphysik der Sitten, gesammelte Schriften (Akademie-Ausgaben), Bd. 6. Berlin
Khaw MW, Grab DA, Livermore MA, Vossler CA, Glimcher PW (2015) The measurement of subjective value and its relation to contingent valuation and environmental public goods. PLoS ONE 10(7):1–19
Kitzmueller M, Shimshack J (2012) Economic perspectives on corporate social responsibility. J Econ Lit 50(1):51–84
Klausner M (1984) Sociological theory and the behavior of financial markets. In: Adler PA, Adler P (eds) The social dynamics of financial markets. JAI Press, Greenwich, CT, pp 57–81
Klein N (2000) No logo: taking aim at the brand bullies. Knopf Canada, Toronto
Knetsch JL, Thaler RH (1986) Fairness and the assumptions of economics. J Bus 59(4):285–300
Knight FH (1921) Risk, uncertainty and profit. Houghton Mifflin, Boston, MA
Knoepfel I (2004) Who cares wins. Connecting financial markets to a changing world. http://www.unepfi.org/fileadmin/events/2004/stocks/who_cares_wins_global_compact_2004.pdf. Accessed 16 Oct 2018
Kogut B, Kulatilaka N (2001) Capabilities as real options. Organ Sci 12(6):744–758
Kogut B, Zander U (1992) Knowledge of the firm, combinative capabilities, and the replication of technology. Organ Sci 3(3):383–397
KPMG (2014) A new vision of value. Connecting corporate and societal value creation. http://www.upj.de/nachrichten_detail.81.0.html?&tx_ttnews[tt_news]=2848&tx_ttnews[backPid]=20&cHash=c0c79d2f9a. Accessed 4 Aug 2018
Kritzman M, Markowitz HM (2017) An interview with Nobel Laureate Harry M. Markowitz. Financ Anal J 73(4):16–21
Kuhn TS (1970) The structure of scientific revolutions, 2nd edn. University of Chicago Press, Chicago, IL
Küpper H-U (2006) Unternehmensethik. Hintergründe, Konzepte, Anwendungen. Schäffer-Poeschel, Stuttgart
Kyläheiko K, Sandström J, Virkkunen V (2002) Dynamic capability view in terms of real options. Int J Prod Econ 80(1):65–83
Lintner J (1965) The valuation of risk assets and the selection of risky investments in stock portfolios and capital budgets. Rev Econ Stat 47(1):13–37
Louche C (2004) Ethical investment: process and mechanism of institutionalisation in the Netherlands, 1990–2002. Doctoral Thesis, Erasmus University, Rotterdam

Lusardi A, Tufano P (2009) Debt Literacy, Financial Experiences, and Overindebtedness. NBER Working Paper 14808. Auf den Seiten von: Natl Bur Econ Res (NBER). http://www.nber.org/papers/w14808. Accessed 12 Oct 2018

Lutz F, Lutz V (1951) The theory of investment of the firm. Greenwood Press, New York

Maaß F, Chlosta S, Icks A. Welter F (2014) Konzepte und Wirkungen nachhaltigen. Unternehmertums (Concepts and Effects of Sustainable Management), IfM-Materialien Nr. 227, Institut fuer Mittelstandsforschung. http://www.ifm-bonn.org//uploads/tx_ifmstudies/IfM-Materialien-227.pdf. Accessed 4 Aug 2018

Mahoney JT, Pandian JR (1992) The resource-based view within the conversation of strategic management. Strateg Manag J 13(5):363–380

Marglin SA (1963) The social rate of discount and the optimal rate of investment. Q J Econ 77 (1):95–11

Margolis JD, Walsh JP (2003) Misery loves companies: rethinking social initiatives by business. Adm Sci Q 48(2):268–305

Markowitz H (1952) Portfolio selection. J Financ 7(1):77–91

Mason CL, Wilson RM (2000) Conceptualising financial literacy. Res Ser Pap 7. https://dspace.lboro.ac.uk/dspacejspui/ bitstream/2134/ 2016/3/2000-7.pdf, Accessed 25 July 2018

McGuire JW (1963) Business and society. McGraw-Hill, New York

McKenzie L (1959) On the existence of general equilibrium for a competitive economy. Econometrica 27(1):54–71

McWilliams A, Siegel D (1997) Event studies in management research: theoretical and empirical issues. Acad Manag J 40(3):626–657

Meadows DL (2009) Unsere Systeme sind nicht schockresistent ("Our Systems are not resilient"). Interview given in "Finanz und Wirtschaft" 98: 25

Meadows DH, Meadows DL, Randers J, Behrens WW (1973) The limits to growth. Universe Books, New York

Meadows DH, Randers J, Meadows DL (2009) The limits to growth: the 30-year update. Chelsea Green, White River Junction, VT

Mill JS (1863) Utilitarianism. Parker, Son and Bourn, London

Modigliani F (1963) The monetary mechanism and its interaction with real phenomena. Rev Econ Stat 65(1):79–110

Modigliani F, Miller MH (1958) The cost of capital, corporate finance and the theory of investments. Am Econ Rev 48(3):261–297

Monks RAG, Minow N (1995) Corporate governance. Blackwell, Cambridge, MA

Moskowitz M (1972) Choosing socially responsible stocks. Bus Soc 1:71–75

Mossin JF (1966) Equilibrium in a capital asset market. Econometrica 34:768–783

Muth JF (1961) Rational expectations and the theory of price. Econometrica 29(6):315–335

Myers SC (1977) Determinants of corporate borrowing. J Financ Econ 5(2):147–176

New Climate Economy (2016) The sustainable infrastructure imperative: financing for better growth and development. The 2016 new climate economy report. http://newclimateeconomy.report/2016/wp-content/uploads/sites/4/2014/08/NCE_2016Report.pdf. Accessed 4 Aug 2018

Nordhaus WD, Tobin J (1972) Is growth obsolete? vol 96. National Bureau of Economic Research, New York http://www.nber.org/chapters/c3621. Accessed 6 Oct 2018

O'Hara M (1995) Market microstructure theory. Blackwell, Cambridge, MA

OECD (2003) Emerging systemic risks – final report to the OECD futures project, Paris

OECD (2016) Development co-operation report 2016: the sustainable development goals as business opportunities. https://doi.org/10.1787/dcr-2016-en. Accessed 4 Aug 2018

Ostroy JM (1973) The informational efficiency of monetary exchange. Am Econ Rev 63 (4):597–610

Paul CM, Siegel D (2006) Corporate social responsibility and economic performance. J Prod Anal 26(3):207–211

Pava ML, Krausz J (1996) the association between corporate social responsibility and financial performance: the paradox of social cost. J Bus Ethics 15(3):321–357

Pearce D, Atkinson G (1998) The concept of sustainable development: an evaluation of its usefulness ten years after Brundtland. Swiss J Econ Stat 134(3):251–269

Pelsmacker P, Driese L, Rayp G (2005) Do consumers care about ethics? Willingness to pay for fair-trade coffee. J Consum Aff 39(2):363–385

Penrose ET (1959) The theory of the growth of the firm. Oxford University Press, Oxford

Picketty T (2014) Capital in the twenty-first century. Belknap Press of Harvard University Press, Cambridge, MA

Pigou AC (2002) Wealth and welfare, revised version of AC Pigou, Wealth and Welfare (1912). Macmillan, London

Post J (2000) Moving from geographic to virtual communities: global corporate citizenship in a Dot.com world. Bus Soc Rev 105(1):26–46

PWC (2016) Integrated reporting in Germany: The Dax 30 benchmark survey 2015. https://www.pwc.de/de/rechnungslegung/assets/studie-integrated-reporting-2015.pdf. Accessed 6 Sept 2018

Raines JP, Leathers CG (1994) Financial derivative instruments and social ethics. J Bus Ethics 13:197–204

Rappaport A (2006) Ten ways to create shareholder value. Harv Bus Rev 84:237–242

Rawls J (1971) A theory of justice. Belknap Press of Harvard University Press, Cambridge, MA

Reed DJ (2001) Stalking the elusive business case for corporate sustainability. World Resources Institute, Washington, D.C.

Reimsbach D, Hahn R, Gürtürk A (2017) Integrated Reporting and Assurance of Sustainability Information: an Experimental Study on Professional Investors' Information Processing. Eur Account Rev:1–23. https://doi.org/10.1080/09638180.2016.1273787

Renn O, Klinke A (2004) Systemic risks: a new challenge for risk management. EMBO Rep 5 (Suppl. 1):41–S46

Revelli C, Viviani J-L (2015) Financial performance of socially responsible investing (SRI): what have we learned? A meta-analysis. Bus Ethics Eur Rev 24(2):158–185

Ross SA (1976) The arbitrage theory of capital asset pricing. J Econ Theory 13(2):341–360

Ross SA (1978) Some notes on financial incentive-signalling models, activity choice and risk preferences. J Financ 23(3):777–794

Rost K, Ehrmann T (2015) Reporting biases in empirical management research: the example of win-win corporate social responsibility. Bus Soc 54(1):1–49

Russo MV, Fouts PA (1997) A resource-based perspective on corporate environmental performance and profitability. Acad Manag J 40(3):534–559

Rychen DS, Salganik LH (2003) A holistic model of competence. In: Rychen DS, Salganik LH (eds) Key competencies for a successful life and a well-functioning society. Huber Publishers, Ashland, OH

Salzmann AJ (2013) The integration of sustainability into the theory and practice of finance: an overview of the state of the art and outline of future developments. J Bus Econ 83(6):555–576

Samuelson PA (1968) What classical and neoclassical theory really was. Can J Econ 1(1):1–15

Samuelson PA (1971) Love that corporation. Mountain Bell Magazine, Spring

Samuelson PA (1998) How foundations came to be. J Econ Lit 36:1375–1386

Sandberg J, Juravle C, Hedesström TM, Hamilton I (2009) The heterogeneity of socially responsible investment. J Bus Ethics 87:519–533

Sanford CS (1993) Financial markets in 2020. Federal Reserve Bank of Kansas City symposium. https://www.kansascityfed.org/publicat/sympos/1993/s93sanfo.pdf. Accessed 6 Sept 2018

Schäfer H (2009) Corporate social responsibility rating. In: Aras G, Crowther D (eds) A handbook of corporate governance and corporate social responsibility. Gower Publishing, Surrey, pp 449–465

Schäfer, H (2012) Sustainable finance. A conceptual outline, University of Stuttgart, BWI/Abt. III, Working Paper Series, No. 03/2012. http://ssrn.com/author=432903. Accessed 6 Sept 2018

Schäfer H (2018) Germany: the 'greenhorn' in the green finance revolution. Environ Sci Policy Sustain Dev 60(1):18–27. https://doi.org/10.1080/00139157.2018.1397472 Accessed 6 Sept 2018

Schäfer H, Goldschmidt R (2010) Corporate social responsibility of large family owned firms in germany: conceptual outline and empirical results. Special issue "family firms". Int J Entrep Small Bus 11(3):285–307

Schäfer H, Sörensen D (2010) Creating options while designing prototypes – value management in the automobile industry reconsidered. J Manuf Technol Manag 21(6):721–742

Schäfer H, Völker F (2018) Socially driven stakeholder networks of German family-owned companies as enablers of economic success – a theoretical and empirical study. In: Altenurger R (ed) Innovation management and corporate social responsibility, CSR, Sustainability, Ethics & Governance. Springer, Heidelberg, pp 309–333

Schmalenbach E (1922) Finanzierungen, vol 3. Akademische Verlagsgesellschaft, Leipzig

Schmidheiny S, Zorraquin FJL (1996) Financing change: the financial community, eco-efficiency, and sustainable development. MIT, Cambridge, MA

Schneider F (2002) The hidden financial flows of Islamic Terrorist Organisations: some preliminary results from an economic perspective. Discussion Paper, Department of Economics, University of Linz, Austria, presented at "The Economic Consequences of Global Terrorism", DIW, Berlin, 14–15 June 2002

Schneider F (2013) The financial flows of transnational crime and tax fraud in OECD countries. What do we (not) know. Public Financ Rev 41(5):677–707

Schneider, F, Caruso R (2011) The (hidden) financial flows of terrorist and transnational crime organizations: a literature review and some preliminary empirical results. Economics of Security Working Paper 52, Berlin: Economics of Security. https://core.ac.uk/download/pdf/6774806.pdf. Accessed 6 Sept 2018

Scholtens B (2006) Finance as a driver of corporate social responsibility. J Bus Ethics 68(1):19–33

Scholtens B, Sievännen R (2012) Drivers of socially responsible investing: a case study of four Nordic countries. J Bus Ethics 115(3):605–615

Schröder M (2014) Financial effects of corporate social responsibility: a literature review. J Sustain Financ Invest 4(4):337–350

Schwartz MS, Saiia D (2012) Should firms go "beyond profits"? Milton Friedman versus Broad CSR. Bus Soc Rev 117(1):1–31

Sedlacek T (2011) Economics of good and evil. The quest of economic meaning from Gilgamesh to Wall Street. Oxford University Press, New York

Sen A (1987) On ethics and economics. Blackwell, Oxford

Sen A (1993) Money and value. On the ethics and economics of finance. Econ Philos 9(2):203–207

Shah AK (1997) The social dimensions of financial risk. J Financ Regul Compliance 5(3):195–207

Sharpe WF (1964) Capital asset prices: a theory of market equilibrium under conditions of risk. J Financ 19:442–452

Shiller RJ (2003) From efficient markets theory to bounded rationality. J Econ Perspect 17 (1):83–104

Shionoya Y (2001) The German Historical School: the historical and ethical approach to economics. Routledge, London

Siddiq MN (1995) An overview of public borrowing in early Islamic history. J Islamic Econ Stud 2 (2):61–78

Simnett R (1996) The effect of information selection, information processing and task complexity on predictive accuracy on auditors. Acc Organ Soc 21(7/8):699–719. https://doi.org/10.1016/0361-3682(96)00006-2

Simon HA (1955) A behavioral model of rational choice. Quarterly Journal of Economics 69 (1):99–118

Smith A (1776) An inquiry into the nature and cause of wealth of nations. W. Strahan and T. Cadell, London

Solomon E (1963) The theory of financial management. Columbia University Press, New York

Soppe A (2000) Finance and ethics, Erasmus University Rotterdam. Dissertation, Dept. of Finance. Rotterdam

Soppe A (2004) Sustainable corporate finance. J Bus Ethics 53(2):213–224

Southwood P (2003) Shareholder engagement: prospects for improving corporate social responsibility. Int J Bus Perform Manag 5(2/3):223–236
Sparkes R, Cowton CJ (2004) The maturing of socially responsible investment: a review of the developing link with corporate social responsibility. J Bus Ethics 52(1):45–57
Stern NH (2007) The economics of climate change – the Stern review. Cambridge University Press, Cambridge, MA
Stern NH (2009) The global deal – climate change and the creation of a new era of progress and prosperity. PublicAffairs, New York
Stiglitz J (1974) Growth with exhaustible natural resources: efficient and optimal growth paths. Rev Econ Stud 41 (128) (Special Issue): 123–137
Stiglitz J (2013) The price of inequality: how the today's divided society endangers our future, and what can be done. W. W. Norton & Company, New York
Stulz R (2000) Why risk management is not rocket science. Financial Times, 3–5 London
Sturgess GL, Cumming LM, Dicker J, Sotiropoulos A, Sultan N (2011) Payment by outcome, a commissioner's toolkit. The 2020 Public Services Trust at the RSA, London
Swain MR, Haka SF (2000) Effects of information load on capital budgeting decisions. Behav Res Account 12:171–198
Talaulicar T (2010) The concept of the balanced company and its implications for corporate governance. Soc Bus Rev 5(3):232–244
Taleb N (2007) The black swan. Random House, New York
Task Force on Climate-Related Financial Disclosures (TCFD) (2016) Recommendations of the task force on climate-related financial disclosures. https://www.fsb-tcfd.org/publications/recommendations-report/. Accessed 9 Sept 2018
Taylor T (2014) Economics and Morality. Finance Dev 51:34–38
Teece DJ, Pisano G, Shuen A (1997) Dynamic capabilities and strategic management. Strateg Manag J 18(7):509–533
Tett A (2005) Market faith goes out the window as the 'model monkeys' lose track of reality. Financial Times New York. 23
The Economist Intelligence Unit (2015) The cost of inaction. Recognising the value at risk from climate change. http://www.economistinsights.com/financial-services/analysis/cost-inaction. Accessed 9 Sept 2018
Tirole J (2001) Corporate governance. Econometrica 69(1):1–35
Tobin J (1958) Liquidity preferences as behavior towards risk. Rev Econ Stud 25(1):65–86
Tobin J (1970) Money and income: Post Hoc Ergo Propter Hoc? Q J Econ 84(2):301–317
UNCTAD (2015) Investing in sustainable development goals. Action plan for private investments in SDGs. http://unctad.org/en/PublicationsLibrary/osg2015d3_ en.pdf. Accessed 4 Aug 2018
UNEP (2011) Towards a green economy: pathways to sustainable development and poverty eradication – a synthesis for policy makers. https://sustainabledevelopment.un.org/index.php?page=view&type=400&nr=126&menu=1515. Accessed 9 Sept 2018
UNEP (2015) The financial system we need. The UNEP inquiry report. Aligning the financial system with sustainable development. http://apps.unep.org/publications/index.php?option=com_pub&task=download&file=011830_en. Accessed 20 Aug 2018
UNEP FI (2010) Universal ownership – why environmental externalities matter to institutional investors, Geneva. http://www.unepfi.org/fileadmin/documents/universal_ownership_full.pdf. Accessed 9 Sept 2018
UNEP FI (2013) PORTFOLIO CARBON – measuring, disclosing and managing the carbon intensity of investments and investment portfolios. Report der UNEP FI Climate Change Advisory Group und der UNEP FI Investment Commission. http://www.unepfi.org/fileadmin/climatechange/UNEP_FI_Investor_Briefing_Portfolio_Carbon.pdf. Accessed 9 Sept 2018
UNEP FI (2018) Extending our horizons: assessing credit risk and opportunity in a changing climate, part I: transition-related risks and opportunities. http://www.unepfi.org/publications/banking-publications/extending-our-horizons/. Accessed 9 Sept 2018
Unger B (2013) Can money laundering decrease? Public Financ Rev 41(5):658–676

United Nations Framework Convention on Climate Change (UNFCC) (1998) Kyoto protocol to the United Nations Framework Convention on Climate Change. https://unfccc.int/sites/default/files/kpeng.pdf. Accessed 9 Sept 2018

United Nations Framework Convention on Climate Change (UNFCCC) (2010) Report of the conference of the parties on its sixteenth session, held in Cancun from 29 November to 10 December 2010. http://unfccc.int/resource/docs/2010/cop16/eng/07a01.pdf#page=17. Accessed 4 Aug 2018

Vogel D (2010) The private regulation of global corporate conduct. Achievements and limitations. Bus Soc 49(1):68–87

Vorrath J, Beisheim M (2015) Organised crime in the "2030 agenda for sustainable development". Berlin: Stiftung Wissenschaft und Politik (SWP). Deutsches Institut für Internationale Politik und Sicherheit. http://nbn-resolving.de/urn:nbn:de:0168-ssoar-450382. Accessed 9 Sept 2018

Waddock S (2009) The social contract of business in society. In: Aras G, Crowther D (eds) A handbook of corporate governance and corporate social responsibility. Gower Publishing, Surrey, pp 69–82

Waddock SA, Graves SB (1997) The corporate social performance-financial performance link. Strateg Manag J 18(4):303–319

Weber O, Scholz R, Michalik G (2010) Incorporating sustainability criteria into credit risk management. Bus Strateg Environ 19:39–50

Wernerfelt B (1984) A resource-based view of the firm. Strateg Manag J 5(2):171–180

Weston JF (1966) The scope and methodology of finance. Prentice-Hall, Englewood Cliffs, NJ

White LH (2008) Menger, Carl (1840–1921). In: Hamowy R (ed) The encyclopedia of libertarianism. Sage, Thousand Oaks, CA, pp 325–326

Williams JB (1938) The theory of investment. Harvard University Press, Cambridge, MA

World Bank (2012) Turn down the heat – why a 4°C warmer world must be avoided. http://climatechange.worldbank.org/sites/default/files/Turn_Down_the_heat_Why_a_4_degree_centrigrade_warmer_world_must_be_avoided.pdf. Accessed 4 Aug 2018

World Commission on Environment and Development (1987) Our common future. http://www.unric.org/html/german/entwicklung/rio5/brundtland/A_42_427.pdf. Accessed 4 Aug 2018

Zadek S (2004) The path to corporate responsibility. Harv Bus Rev 12(2):125–132

Zingales L (2000) In search of new foundations. J Financ 55(4):1623–1653

MIX
Papier aus verantwortungsvollen Quellen
Paper from responsible sources
FSC® C105338

If you have any concerns about our products,
you can contact us on
ProductSafety@springernature.com

In case Publisher is established outside the EU,
the EU authorized representative is:
Springer Nature Customer Service Center GmbH
Europaplatz 3, 69115 Heidelberg, Germany

Printed by Libri Plureos GmbH
in Hamburg, Germany